THE OLD MINE ROAD

Charles Gilbert Hine on the Old Mine Road where it swings around the foot of Council Hill.

The
OLD MINE ROAD

by

C. G. HINE

Introduction by Henry Charlton Beck

RUTGERS UNIVERSITY PRESS

New Brunswick *New Jersey*

Fourth printing, 1985

Manufactured in the United States of America

Library of Congress Cataloging in Publication Data

Hine, Charles Gilbert, 1859–1931.
The Old Mine Road, Intro. by Henry Charlton Beck.

171 p.

Illus.

First published in 1908 under title: History and legend.
1. Old Mine Road. 2. Minisink region—Hist.
I. Title
F127.M5H5 1963 974.73 63-15524
ISBN 0-8135-0427-9 (pbk.)

INTRODUCTION TO THE 1963 PRINTING

There is always at least one adventure associated with the discovery of an unusual and rare book. I am more than happy to tell you that a series of adventures introduced me not only to *History and Legend, Fact, Fancy and Romance of the Old Mine Road, Kingston, N. Y., to the Mine Holes of Pahaquarry* but also to some of the memories of its author, Charles Gilbert Hine, the kind of man I wish I could have known in person.

The book, first published as *Hine's Annual,* 1908, is a most important and delightful story of what must be, without question, the first commercial road in this country, a road so ancient that we can only surmise that it was built by very early Dutch settlers intent on exploiting the mineral wealth of the Minisink Country, of which rumors had circulated since the voyage of Henry Hudson. And yet, until the step-by-step adventures began, almost as in a detective story, I had heard of the Hine book only in passing.

A book about the old road that I did know was *That Ancient Trail* (*The Old Mine Road*) by Amelia Stickney Decker, who set out to record the stories of the early inhabitants of the settlements along the road and preserve a pictorial record of the old houses and inns and churches still standing. I well remember journeying to the home of the late Mrs. Decker to obtain an autographed copy—and then visiting most of the wonderful places revealed in text and photograph. In fact, so important had this work become in my estimation, and in the light of reports that the coming upper Delaware River reservoirs might obliterate folklore and history in large areas from Port Jervis down, that I inquired about a reissue. I was pleased to learn that the book, published privately by the author first in 1942, was on its way to a third printing, in limited edition, by my friends at the Trenton Printing Company.

My adventures with the Hine book began at an auction. James M. Ransom, whose Wall Street wisdom blends with that of another kind in his researches among the abandoned iron mines of the Ramapos, called me one day to report that two of my books were on the list of a well-known book auction gallery, something that rarely has happened. I was interested in one because it was a first edition of my first book of nonfiction, *Forgotten Towns of Southern New Jersey,* which had vanished mysteriously from my library. Gallery authorities assured me that a high bid might bring my "first-born" home but that a lower figure might take the second, *Fare to Midlands* (reissued in 1962 as *The Jersey Midlands*). I missed the *Midlands* book—but that is beside the point. The point is that Jim Ransom also had mentioned Charles Gilbert Hine's Old Mine Road book, in which he said he thought I might be interested.

Much to my surprise, even though the family treasury was depleted, with an advance birthday gift as an excuse, I became the owner of *History and Legend, Fact, Fancy and Romance of the Old Mine Road,* which, with the full title of its day, should surely be set to music. Even a hasty scanning assured me that all the lore of an old road—the mystery, the wonder, and the forgotten history, which in a later day the Deckers and the Daughters of the American Revolution had succeeded in preserving in part—was there.

Alarmed all over again that so many old houses and forts with markers to identify what they were might lie, sooner than anyone dreamed, at the bottom of a watery grave, I hurried off to see William Sloane, director of the Rutgers University Press. Here, I said, was a rich sector of early America which must be reclaimed by New Jersey, on paper at least, for the Tercentenary Year. I mention Bill Sloane, for he it was who inspired most of the Charles Gilbert Hine adventures that followed.

I was asked to write an introduction and, at the same time, try to discover, or recover, all I could about Charles Gilbert Hine—who, to me by now, I must tell you, is one of the least honored of New Jersey's unassuming but distinguished writers. First I called on Jim Ransom, who had begun it all. Then I consulted Donald A. Sinclair, curator of Special Collections of the Rutgers University Library; Miss Miriam V. Studley, principal librarian of the New Jersey Division of the Newark Public Library; and John Bohne Ehrhardt, of Madison, formerly publisher of the Madison *Eagle.*

First let me say that, based on what they have told me and what I have pried out on my own, Charles Gilbert must have been a kindred soul. I say again that I wish that I could have known him. But it turned out that I was over thirty years too late. Although Mr. Sinclair could tell me that Charles Gilbert Hine was born in 1859, his records gave no date of death, so it took more research to find out that he died in East Orange on June 6, 1931. Almost at once, we came upon obituaries in the Newark *Evening News* for Saturday, June 6, 1931, and in the New York *Times* and Newark *Sunday Call* for Sunday, the day following. They told little, but did provide an address: "Hine, at East Orange, N. J., on Saturday, June 6, 1931, Charles Gilbert

Hine, husband of Sarah Avery Hine at 164 Harrison Street, East Orange. Interment private." All the while, I must confess at this point, the title of another book, *Woodside, the North End of Newark, N. J.*, began to gnaw at my memory. Furthermore, the series title, *Hine's Annual,* on my Old Mine Road book, led me to suspect that Mr. Hine must have written other books on local history.

Jim Ransom had said tersely that Charles Gilbert had walked up one side of the Hudson River, and then had written about it; walking up the other side later, he repeated the performance. John Ehrhardt wrote in his usual way: "I have some of the information you need on Charles Gilbert Hine," he said. "He was a Newark boy, grew up in Woodside, north of Newark near the Belleville line, and I know that he produced a very fine book on Woodside. Hine's father was Charles Cole Hine, long a civic and church leader in the neighborhood. His mother was active in charities and once served as president of the home for incurables.

"Charles Cole Hine was born in New Haven, Connecticut, December 12, 1825, moved to Hornell, New York, when he was six, later was taken to Massillon, Ohio, by his parents. He was an early telegrapher and followed the lines westward. He was in St. Louis when he married Mary Hazard Avery July 4, 1853. Charles Gilbert would appear to have been their eldest son, if not their oldest child." (Deaconess Nathalie E. Winser was to correct this assumption later.) "Charles Cole Hine shortly went to the wall, as we say now, operating a female seminary in New Albany, Indiana, and he had to go back to his previous occupation of selling insurance. He was quite successful and became a general agent in charge of opening up the hinterland for the Aetna

Insurance Company. In 1868 he became owner and editor of the *Insurance Monitor* in New York City.

"For the better part of a year the family lived in boarding-houses while their home was being built. Inasmuch as Charles Gilbert was born in 1859, it would appear that he lived in Woodside from the time he was eight. I have seen a letter written by Charles Gilbert Hine in about 1907. The stationery says only this: C. G. Hine, 100 William Street, New York City. The old directories show that this was the address of the *Insurance Monitor* and that Charles Gilbert was his father's successor as editor."

When the journal changed ownerhip in 1920, having been in the Hine family for half a century, one of the leading insurance journalists, Clarence Axman, pointed out that the "famous old *Monitor* was supreme in the days of personalities," when insurance journals played an important role in the internal fights in the business.

"The different editors, some of whom were brilliant writers, lined up for or against companies or individuals in controversies, and then went the limit in their columns, much in the fashion of writers in the daily papers of the period when Mark Twain was a reporter in Nevada and James Gordon Bennett, the elder, shook a wicked pen. One of the principal protagonists and hardest fighters was the late C. C. Hine, editor of the *Monitor,* a man of wide and varied experience in the insurance business and journalism, a trenchant writer."

When C. C. Hine died in 1897, his sons incorporated the Hine Insurance Publishing Company, which company published the *Insurance Monitor, The Insurance Law Journal,* and the *Workmen's Compensation Law Journal,* as well as several insurance guides and directories. Apparently the

Insurance Monitor had become so famous that in 1922 the new owners, after a brief interval of publishing it as the *American Insurance Digest,* compromised by calling it *American Insurance Digest (and Insurance Monitor)*—and this is the name under which it survives today.

From Harry S. Weeks, chief librarian of the Insurance Society of New York, I found out that Charles Gilbert Hine was also his father's successor as the head of the Underwriters and Credit Bureau, Inc., an organization built up by Hine the elder to collect financial and hazard information to protect underwriters all over the country from getting caught on fraudulent claims. Charles Gilbert was regarded by private business, the police, and even the federal government as an expert on smelling out a bad risk, and his organization as a mine of loss-saving information.

How such a busy and prominent man in the insurance world found time to pursue antiquarian inquiries, and write about them, I do not know unless it was that the complete change gave him a special energy and a kind of relaxation few of us know. Be that as it may, there can be no doubt that Charles Gilbert had a deep and abiding interest in history and legend as well as the natural beauty of the countryside around him, wherever he was. In all he published about a dozen books, nine of them bearing the series title of *Hine's Annual.* Each of the *Annuals,* which appeared from 1905-1914, usually covered one area or subject that had interested him and all appear to have been privately printed in small editions. The 1906 *Annual* contains the information: "Privately printed. This edition is limited to 52 copies." The 1907 *Annual* announces wryly, "This edition is limited to such copies as can be given away. Each and every copy being numbered one." Mr. Hine was a skillful amateur photographer, and some of the *Annuals* are elaborately illustrated with hand-colored chloride or platinum prints tipped into the pages. The *Annuals* perhaps could be classed as hobby publications except for one thing—their value this long after makes it evident, at least to me, that Mr. Hine regarded his researches as more than that, chronicles of questioning to be recounted with care. It was almost as if the author remained faithful to two vocations, probably more.

The following is a listing of Charles Gilbert Hine's books taken from the Library of Congress Catalogue.

History and Legend, Fact, Fancy and Romance of the Old Mine Road, Kingston, N. Y., to the Mine Holes of Pahaquarry . . . [New York?] 1908. *Hine's Annual,* 1908.

History and Legend of Howard Avenue and the Serpentine Road, Grymes Hill, Staten Island, Gathered by Charles Gilbert Hine from Real Estate Records and Long Memories . . . [New York? Priv. print., Hine Brothers printery, 1914] *Hine's Annual,* 1914.

The History of Cedar Neck [Martha's Vineyard] *Set to Words by C. G. Hine.* [n. p.] Priv. print., 1907. *Hine's Annual,* 1907.

The House That Tom Built, Showing Why, How, When and Where This House Was Erected. Including Elaborate Working Details of the Methods Used in Securing the Site; the Construction of the Building; Impartial Notes on the Architect; an Opinion of the Furnace Man; and Other Interesting and Valuable Suggestions for Those about to Select a Home. [New York?] *Hine's Annual,* 1910. The house was on Howard Avenue, Grymes Hill, Staten Island, and Tom was Thomas Avery Hine, architect.

Legends, Stories and Folklore of Old Staten Island, by

Charles Gilbert Hine and William T. Davis. [New York] Staten Island Historical Society [1947—]. Part I. *The North Shore.*

The New York and Albany Post Road, from Kings Bridge to "the Ferry at Crawlier, over against Albany," Being an Account of a Jaunt on Foot Made at Sundry Convenient Times between May and November, Nineteen Hundred and Five, by C. G. Hine. New York, C. G. Hine, 1905. Published also as *Hine's Annual,* 1905, Book I [Newark? N. J., 1906].

The Story and Documentary History of the Perine House, Dongan Hills, Staten Island, Headquarters of the Staten Island Antiquarian Society. [New York?] Staten Island Antiquarian Society, Inc., 1915.

The Story of Martha's Vineyard, from the Lips of Its Inhabitants, Newspaper Files and Those Who Have Visited Its Shores, Including Stray Notes on Local History and Industries; Collected and Arranged by C. G. Hine and Illustrated by C. G. and Thos. A. Hine. New York, Hine Brothers [1908].

Travels in Nova Scotia in the Year 1913; Containing Much That Is Curious Concerning the Manners and Customs of the People. The Stories and Legends of the Southern Shore and Including Short Excursions into the History of the Country. [New York? 1913] *Hine's Annual,* 1913.

The West Bank of the Hudson River, Albany to Tappan; Notes on Its History and Legends, Its Ghost Stories and Romances. Gathered by a Wayfaring Man Who May Now and Then Have Erred Therein. [Newark? N. J., 1907.] *Hine's Annual,* 1906.

Woodside, the North End of Newark, N. J.; Its History, Legends and Ghost Stories, Gathered from the Records and the Older Inhabitants Now Living. [New York? 1909.]

Hine's Annual, 1909.

Edith White Lawrence. *The Fourth Tour of Doctor Syntax in Search of View; Being a True and Dependable Account of the Adventures and Discoveries Made by This Famous Traveler on the Hill of Grymes, U.S.A., and Including Brief Notes Showing His Extreme Domestic Felicity*, by Miss Edith White Lawrence, ably assisted by Doctor Hicks Syntax Lawrence and Mr. Charles Gilbert Hine . . . [New York? 1912?] *Hine's Annual*, 1911-1912.

The Staten Island Historical Society possesses two other Hine books and an unbound, undated cookbook:

A Happy Adventure (New-found-land). Log of the First Cruise of the Sarah H. Newly Launched on the Sea of Matrimony as Written by the First Mate. Privately printed for C. G. Hine. [1915?]

History, Story and Legend of Old King's Highway. 1916

The House of Hine Presents . . . Unbound Cookbook of Gathered Recipes.

John Ehrhardt has told me that "C.G." was also the author of a whimsical ode to the Staten Island crab, but, even without this, the list of neglected Americana is impressive.

It was Bill Sloane who insisted that there must be someone, somewhere, who had known Charles Gilbert Hine and could tell us what, as a person as well as a craftsman, he really was like. Unfortunately, I found no one who could help me in East Orange, for neighborhood changes had come to Harrison Street, and the name Hine was unknown to all those for whom I phrased the customary questions. However, inquiry of the Staten Island Historical Society produced a letter from Mrs. Hildegard J. Safford, the librarian, in which she gave me not only a list of the Hine books in the society's collections but also a copy of the obituary that appeared in the Staten Island *Advance*. From the latter, I discovered that the Antiquarian Society, of which Mr. Hine was a founder, had been instrumental in the preservation of the old Perine House on Richmond Road, and that he was regarded as one of the island's leading historians. He held membership in the Staten Island Institute of Arts and Sciences from 1910.

At this point I suddenly remembered that an old friend, William Lynn McCracken, Sr., had a lively interest in the Richmondtown restoration on Staten Island, and furthermore was old enough to have known Mr. Hine. Mr. McCracken did indeed remember Mr. Hine from his lectures and urged me to come over for a visit and a tour of historic houses on the island. Both he and Miss Dorothy Valentine Smith, a leading member of the historical society, were sure that Mr. Hine had been a long-time resident of the island, and they took me past "the house that Tom built," that is, the house overlooking the bay and harbor entrance designed by Charles Gilbert's brother Thomas Avery. (They told me that the house was now a property of the Roman Catholic Church.)

Thinking back to the lectures, Mr. McCracken said, "Mr. Hine was a grand old man, and his manner reminded me of what that of St. Francis might have been—he loved the outdoors and everything and everybody in it."

On the edge of concluding with this magnificent appraisal, I was told where I might find a friend and former neighbor of Mr. Hine's, Deaconess Nathalie E. Winser of the Episcopal Diocese of Newark, sister of the late Beatrice Winser, long esteemed as a librarian in Newark. I called on Miss Nathalie twice but was told she was not at home, more than likely because she was in the process of moving. Declining to interrupt her work at St. Luke's, Montclair, where she was a member of the staff, I wrote her a letter. Days later, I received a six-page reply.

"I have your note about Gilbert Hine," she answered, "and of course I want to help you all I can. I have known the Hines all my life, as Gilbert's father and my father both came to Woodside in 1866, and bought houses that were being built next door to each other." (Miss Winser's father was Henry J. Winser, city editor of the New York *Times* at the end of the last century.) "The Hines lived at 209 Washington Avenue and the Winsers at 201 in Woodside. The Hines had a one-acre estate. . . ." Here Miss Winser repeated some of the family information I have given you already. However, it was she who corrected the impression that Charles Gilbert was the oldest son. "The Hines had three sons," she said, "and Thomas Avery was the oldest, Charles Gilbert next, and then Edward. I know Gilbert's birthday was September 12. He is buried in Mount Pleasant Cemetery in Newark. I was at his funeral in East Orange, which, as you say, was a private one. Gilbert's father was the owner and publisher of the *Insurance Monitor,* and the office was in William Street, where *Hine's Annuals* were printed and published." Deaconess Winser then listed all of the publications of Gilbert Hine that she knew about, and I noted two that were new to me: *Log of the Totem* and *Mid Depths of Wood Embraced.*

"Gilbert Hine," she went on later, "was married late in life to a distant cousin [Sarah Avery]. All the Hine friends, as far as I know, have died. Both Tom and Gilbert Hine were wonderful photographers, taking the pictures themselves for all their books. Most of the data for the books were gathered by Gilbert on walking and bicycling trips. Gilbert took excellent European pictures, and I wonder what became of them.

"To me one of his most interesting books, as I remember, was *The History of Cedar Neck* (Martha's Vineyard), when the Hines had their summer home there and when the boys were young. Perhaps Gilbert's best-known book is *Woodside,* a history of the upper part of Newark."

Miss Nathalie remembered Charles Gilbert "as a bookish man, bespectacled, who was always thought to be in delicate health." However, he managed to live to the age of seventy-two. I mentioned one of Charles Gilbert's books I had seen with the notation, "Limited Edition." The Deaconess had another of the "C. G." books with these words written on the flyleaf: "This book was printed in a limited edition and all copies are numbered '1.' " This is where a sense of humor comes in.

His *West Bank of the Hudson River,* Miss Studley told me on another occasion, "gives personal glimpses of a very delightful and modest man—for instance: 'I find it far from difficult to get things wrong; that part of the county histories, the histories by towns, from which I must secure my foundation, has in some cases at least a fine reputation for inaccuracy, and the result is that I seem to know many things that are not so.' " Miss Studley regarded Charles Gilbert's *History of Cedar Neck* as "one of the loveliest tributes to a father by a son" she had ever read.

Miss Studley also called my attention to Charles Gilbert Hine's estimate of a preface, actually part of the preface in his Martha's Vineyard book:

"A preface is a thing that few people read, and its use is seldom obvious, but a book without a preface seems like a house without a front hall, with this difference: that while we pass through the front hall, we pass over the preface, and that being the case, there is no use in continuing further."

Actually, there is, because this is my own "front hall" to several rooms in a "house" which is his. In one, Charles Gilbert, too long forgotten, waits to chide me modestly because I forgot his name so quickly when a friend borrowed his *Woodside* and forgot to bring it back; in others, he would like to greet you as one who edited an insurance periodical but devoted his leisure time to inspiring a greater appreciation of areas of New Jersey and New York that he had loved. In this volume he shares his experiences on a walking trip down the one hundred-mile Old Mine Road, stopping time and again to collect history and legend about the people and places as they were in centuries gone by and to describe his delight in the road as he saw it. The Old Mine Road has changed even since his time, and when the bulldozers and other equipment are brought in to build the dams and mountain-top reservoirs, man will have forever obliterated one of his own most fascinating creations.

Henry Charlton Beck

Hillcrest Farm
Robbinsville, New Jersey
January, 1963

THE OLD MINE ROAD

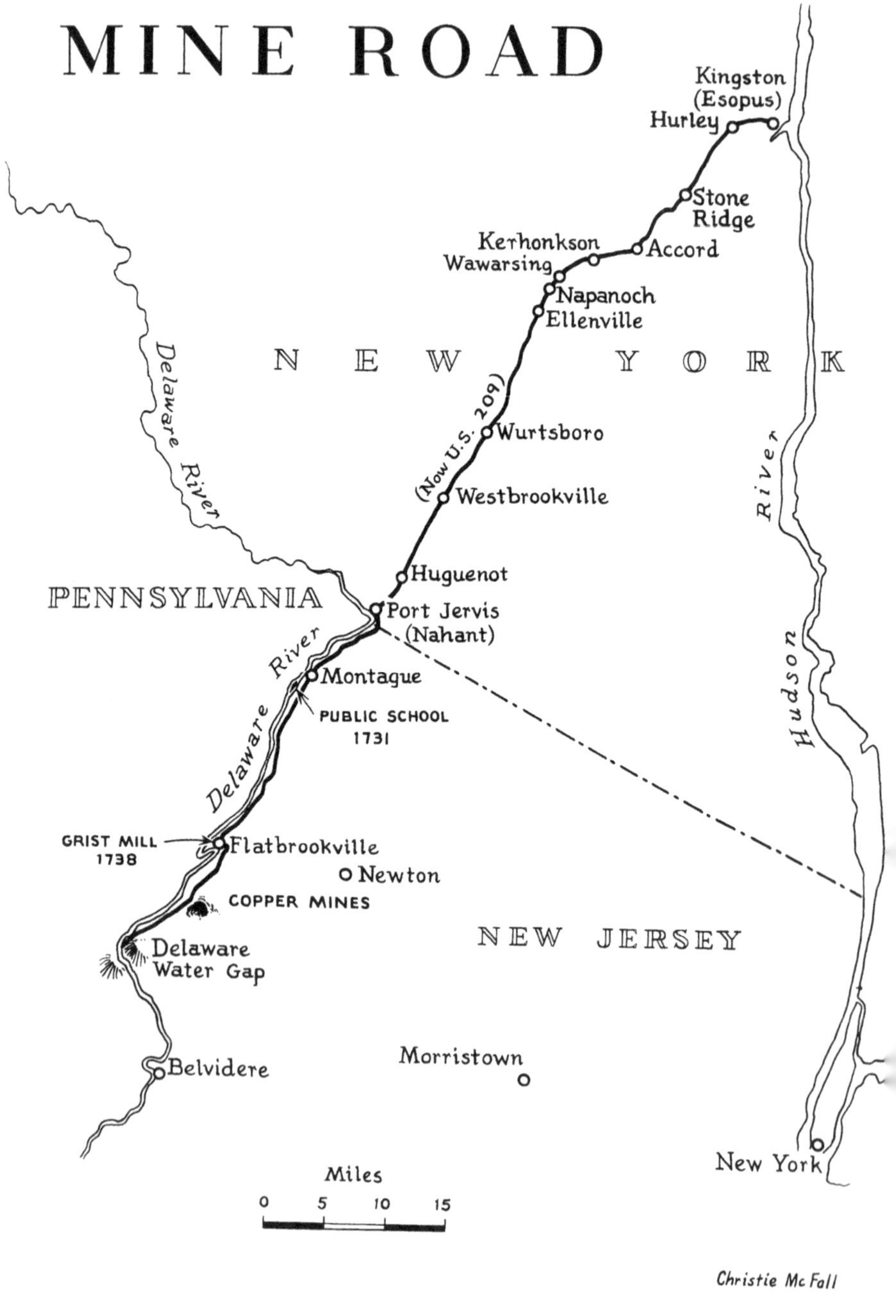

Kingston
(Esopus)
Hurley
Stone
Ridge
Kerhonkson
Accord
Wawarsing
Napanoch
Ellenville
NEW YORK
Delaware River
(Now U.S. 209)
Wurtsboro
Westbrookville
River
Huguenot
PENNSYLVANIA
Port Jervis
(Nahant)
Delaware River
Montague
PUBLIC SCHOOL
1731
Hudson
GRIST MILL
1738
Flatbrookville
Newton
COPPER MINES
NEW JERSEY
Delaware
Water Gap
Morristown
Belvidere
New York
Miles
0 5 10 15

Christie McFall

A FEW FIRST WORDS.

Like the butterfly on the flower-strewn plain, the traveler on foot can laugh at fences or ditches and flit from interest to interest, taking no thought for the highway. Be it a panorama from some hilltop or an old family burial ground in the remote corner of a pasture lot, it is but the storming of a few rails or a bit of barbed wire and a brief walk amid the field flowers, or between rows of growing corn. Hence no excuse is offered for taking this trip on foot; rather do we commend ourself for having selected the best method of travel for the purpose.

It is quite out of the question for the ordinary pen to adequately depict or praise the beauties of such a region as is traversed by our Old Mine Road. A region of mountains and valleys, brooks and waterfalls, country that yields a rich return to the farmer or that is still wild with heaped rock masses, all embroidered with exquisite patterns of mountain and stream and meadowland. All this aside from the richness of its history, its legend and romance.

To be one with such pleasures for a week or more, with no care but to sip from the next cup when the present has sated, to make the few gracious friendships that are part of the experience, to carry home for the long Winter evenings the memory of it all, makes the traveler feel that he has been favored of the gods and has much to be thankful for.

Neither words nor pictures can tell the full story of such a trip as this for, as with Hamlet, the region has "that within which passeth show". One must both see and feel it, have been of it, as only the humble wayfarer can be of it, have stepped from the dusty roadway to the softness of the cool, lush grass, or stood sheltered within the covered bridge while the sudden mountain storm rages down from the heights, and then to step out into the freshness and be part of the gorgeous rolling away of the tattered curtain: ah! tnat indeed is joy unspeakable:—

> "To one who has been long in city pent
> 'T is very sweet to look into the fair
> And open face of Heaven,—to breathe a prayer
> Full in the smile of the blue firmament."
>
> —John Keats.

The facts herein set forth have been freely taken from the writings of those learned in the subject and the lips of those willing to impart information. The fiction is largely due to the author's inability to grasp the truth. But an effort has been made to avoid anything approaching dryness — anyone who has exercised much knows how easy it is to get dry, and how uncomfortable.

It is but fair to acknowledge my indebtedness to Mr. Benjamin M. Brink of Kingston, Dr. George W. Nash of Hurley, Mr John James Schoonmaker of Accord, Mr. David Crist of Wawarsing, Messrs. Demmon Reynolds, Edward Vernoy and Isaiah Rose of Naponoch, Messrs. Thos. H. Benedict, Alfred Ronk, Mr. Taylor and Miss E. H. Gray of Ellenville, Mrs. Harriet G. Brodhead beyond the Leurenkill, Mr. Levi Cuddeback of Cuddebackville, Professor Dolf and Messrs. W. H. Nearpass and Thomas J. Bonnell of Port Jervis, Mr. D. H. Predmore of Brick House, and to many others on whom I made brief calls by the way. While, as usual, thanks are due for the assistance rendered by those in charge of the library of the New York Historical Society, who have placed much that was curious at my disposal, and to those of the Newark Free Library, who have saved me many a weary search.

> "And I'll be sworn 't is true; travellers ne'er did lie,
> Though fools at home condemn 'em."
>
> —Tempest, III., 3.

The Old Mine Road as Hine saw it.

MOTIVE.

In that issue of "Olde Ulster", which appeared for February, 1907, was an article on "The Old Mine Road", which gathered together about all Mr. Brink thought worth recording which in any wise referred to the subject. With that gentleman's permission, I quote his article entire, then follow quotations and condensations from the Sullivan County history, whose author has opinions of his own on the subject; these are again followed by such other matter as I have happened on in my surface scratching.

So much by way of introduction. "Olde Ulster" says:—

"THE OLD MINE ROAD.

"El Dorado, the region of gold, was the quest of centuries succeeding Columbus. Not only among the adventurers who flocked to the Spanish Main, but this was the dream of the colonists of Jamestown and Roanoke. And no sooner had Hudson's discovery revealed 'The River of the Mountaynes' than tales of crystal mountains and wonderful mines aroused adventurous spirits to locate them. The principal object for which the Dutch West India Company was incorporated was not the trade for furs along the Hudson but the capture of the richly laden Spanish fleets with their gold and silver. The trade in furs was but incidental at first.

"The Dutch colonists in the Esopus were agriculturists. But among them there were a few restless and adventurous men who had been interested in the tales told from the first of almost fabulous mines in the interior. These were located as reported in the undefined 'Minisink country'. We will give, chronologically, the story of these reports and speak of the efforts to reach these mines which were situated, in all the accounts, on the Delaware River.

"In the 'Journal of New Netherland' the first golden vision is found under date of 1641. It is

" 'In the interior are pretty high mountains, exhibiting generally strong indications of minerals.'

Four years later (August 31st, 1645,) the West India Company determined to investigate. By this time a definite location is reported of the mine and it is fixed in the Raritan country:—

" 'Having received from savages some specimens of mineral, which we think valuable, and being informed by the savages, that the mountain, from which they had brought the specimens, is situate inland near the Raretang, we have considered it best, most advantageous and profitable for the W. I. Company to use all diligence to discover the said mine and when found and it is valuable, it is resolved to take possession thereof for the said Hon'ble Company and build a fort there.'

"Something of exploration must have been done for in December, 1646, it was reported that

" 'The specimens of New Netherland minerals sent over have been examined but, we are told, no metal has been found in them; we can nevertheless only deem it advisable to order the continuation of the search for minerals by your Honor, and wish to know what kind of metal and this from the innermost, that is the greatest depth, can be obtained; we desire also a description of the place where it is found.'

"For a few years nothing further appears. In 1657 Vice-Director Alrichs, writing of the colony on the Delaware River says:—

"'On this road or way is a good and rich iron mine. * * * situate or contained in a certain mountain near which is a cataract or waterfall on a river which runs past and close by the place, and is adapted to the turning of mills. This river likewise affords facilities for bringing away such substance in a boat.'

"The directors in Holland wrote to Stuyvesant on April 25th, 1659:—

"'We have lately been shown a small piece of mineral, which is said to have come from New Netherland, and which we found to be good and pure copper, so that we have thought it worth while to hear Claes de Ruyter about it, a person who showed that he was not ignorant of it and consequently demonstrated, that a copper mine was said to be in the Nevesinks, also that there was lying between the Manhattans and South-river [Delaware River] a crystal mountain, of which he says he brought several specimens.'

"Claes de Ruyter was not alone as a prospector. In the same letter we read:—

"'Gerrit Jansen Kuyper and Abel de Wolf have also requested us that such lands and minerals may be granted to them (as we conceive situate near the Esopus Kil in and about the high Catskil Mountains).'

"The officials here in New Amsterdam knew nothing of these wonderful discoveries and when they received this letter in July they replied:—

"'We learn with astonishment from your Honor's letter of the report made there by Claes de Ruyter of a coppermine in the Newesinghs and of the request of Gerrit Jansen Kuyper and Abel de Wolf as neither before nor since any communications in this regard have been made to us nor any petition been presented. * * * In the Fall or early next Spring when the woods and hills are burned over and cleared of brushes, and if the good God gives us life, we shall not fail to make inquiries and send your Honors samples of the discovered minerals.'

"The commissioner of the Colony near the mouth of the Delaware took up the matter and made an examination. He reported during the same year (1659) to the authorities in Holland:—

"'We have examined Claes de Ruyter, an old and experienced inhabitant, from whom we have learned thus much, that the reported coppermine does not lie on the South River, but that a crystal mountain was situate between that Colonie and the Manhattans, whereof he himself had brought divers pieces and specimens; furthermore that the acknowledged gold mine was apparently there, for he, having kept house with the Indians living high up the river and about Bachom's country, had understood from them that quicksilver was to be found there.'

"In 1735 Governor Cosby wrote to the London Board of Trade:—

"'In the Jerseys is one extraordinary rich mine and some others are discovered there which afford a good prospect, but in this Province none has yet been discovered tho a good deal of money has been expended in search of them.'

"Having given the stories of the mines from the old documents we propose to tell of the efforts to reach this region of boundless mineral wealth. The spot was near what is now known as 'The Delaware Water Gap' and upon the left bank of the river and thus in New Jersey. No attempt seems to have been made to find a route up the Delaware from its mouth but from the north. It was soon ascertained that access was the easiest from the Esopus, up the valley of the Rondout and to the Delaware along the line on which the engineers of the nineteenth century were to build the Delaware and Hudson Canal. Along this route already pioneers had pushed up from Esopus to Hurley; thence to Marbletown; to Rochester; to Wawarsing; to Peenpack and to Mahackamack, now Port Jervis. Old maps still show the road up the valleys which is reputed to have been the best constructed in the colonies and was known as 'The Old Mine Road'. When it was built no one knows but its course is still shown on maps two hundred years old.

"Hazard's Register contains a copy of a letter written in 1828 by Samuel Preston which throws some light upon the Minisink settlement and, incidentally upon the road to the mines. We will quote therefrom at length:—

" 'In 1787 the writer went on his first surveying tour into Northampton County [Pennsylvania]; he was deputed under John Lukens, Surveyor General and received from him, by way of instructions, the following narrative respecting the settlement of Minisink on the Delaware, above the Kittanny and Blue Mountain:—

" 'That the settlement was formed for a long time before it was known to the Government in Philadelphia. That when the Government was informed of the settlement, they passed a law in 1729 that any such purchases of the Indians should be void; and the purchasers indicted for forcible entry and detainer according to the law of England. That in 1730 they appointed an agent to go and investigate the facts; that the agent so appointed was the famous Surveyor, Nicholas Scull; that he, James Lukens, was N. Scull's apprentice to carry chain and learn surveying. That as they both understood and could talk Indian, they hired Indian guides, and had a fatiguing journey, there being then no white inhabitants in the upper part of Bucks or Northampton County. That they had very great difficulty to lead their horses through the water gap to Minisink flats, which were all settled with Hollanders; with several they could only be understood in Indian. At the venerable Depuis's they found great hospitality and plenty of the necessaries of life. J. Lukens said that the first thing which struck his attention was a grove of apple trees of size far beyond any near Philadelphia. That as N. Scull and himself examined the banks, they were fully of opinion that all those flats had at some very former age been a deep lake before the river broke through the mountain, and that the best interpretation they could make of Minisink was, the water is gone. That S. Dupuis told them when the rivers were frozen he had a good road to Esopus, now Kingston, from the Mine-holes, on the Mine Road, some hundred miles. That he took his wheat and cider there for salt and necessaries, and did not appear to have any knowledge or idea where the river ran—Philadelphia market—or being in the government of Pennsylvania.

" 'They were of opinion that the first settlements of Hollanders in Minisink were many years older than William Penn's charter, and that S. Dupuis had treated them so well they concluded to make a survey of his claim, in order to befriend him if necessary. When they began to survey the Indians gathered around; an old Indian touched Scull and said "Put up string, go home". Then they quit and returned.

" 'I had it in charge from John Lukens to learn more particulars respecting the Mine Road to Esopus, &c. I found Nicholas Dupuis, Esq., son of Samuel, living in a spacious stone house in great plenty and affluence. The old Mineholes were a few miles above, on the Jersey side of the river by the lower point of Paaquarry Flat; that the Minisink settlement extended forty miles or more on both sides of the river. That he had well known the Mine Road to Esopus, and used, before he opened the boat channel through Foul Rife, to drive on it several times every Winter with loads of wheat and cider, as also did his neighbors, to purchase their salt and necessaries in Esopus, having then no other market or knowledge where the river ran to. That after a navigable channel was opened through Foul Rift they generally took to boating, and most of the settlement turned their trade down stream, the Mine Road became less and less traveled.

" 'This interview with the amiable Nicholas Dupuis, Esq., was in June, 1787. He then appeared about sixty years of age. I interrogated as to the particulars of what he knew, as to when and by whom the Mine Road was made, what was the ore they dug and hauled on it, what was the date, and from whence, or how, came the first settlers of Minisink in such great numbers as to take up all the flats on both sides of the river for forty miles. He could only give traditionary accounts of what he had heard from older people, without date, in substance as follows:—

" 'That in some former age there came a company of miners from Holland; supposed, from the great labor expended in making that road, about one hundred miles long, that they were very rich or great people, in working the two mines,—one on the Delaware River where the mountain nearly approaches the lower point of Paaquarry Flat, the other at the north foot of the same mountain, near half way from the Delaware and Esopus. He ever understood that abundance of ore had been hauled on that road, but never could learn whether lead or silver. That the first settlers came from Holland to seek a place of quiet being persecuted for their religion. I believe they were Arminians. They followed the Mine Road to the large flats on the Delaware. That smooth cleared land suited their views. That they bona fide bought the improvements of the native Indians, most of whom then moved to the Susquehanna; that with such as remained there was peace until 1755.

"'I then went to view the Paaquarry Mineholes. There appeared to have been a great abundance of labor done there at some former time, but the mouths of these holes were caved full, and overgrown with bushes. I concluded to myself if there ever had been a rich mine under that mountain it must be there yet in close confinement. The other old men I conversed with gave their traditions similar to N. Dupuis, and they all appeared to be grandsons of the first settlers, and very ignorant as to the dates and things relating to chronology. In the Summer of 1789 I began to build on this place; then came two venerable gentlemen on a surveying expedition. They were the late Gen. James Clinton, the father of the late De Witt Clinton, and Christopher Tappen, Esq., Clerk and Recorder of Ulster County. For many years before they had both been suryevors under General Clinton's father, when he was Surveyor General. In order to learn some history from gentlemen of their general knowledge, I accompanied them in the woods. They both well knew the Mineholes, Mine Road, &c., and as there were no kind of documents or records thereof, united in the opinion that it was a work transacted while the State of New York belonged to the government of Holland; that it fell to the English in 1664; and that the change in government stopped the mining business, and that the road must have been made many years before such digging could have been done. That it undoubtedly must have been the first good road of that extent made in any part of the United States.'

"In the original act creating Ulster County in 1683 it was to extend from Murderers Creek at the Highlands to Sawyers Creek at Saugerties. This line continued to the Delaware River would have left most of the town of Deer Park in Orange County with all of what is now Port Jervis. But provision had been made to prevent this. London Documents XXXI. Col. Hist. VI., page 927, states:—

" 'By an Act of this Colony passed so long ago as the 13th of William the 3rd it is enacted that Maghackemack, and great and little Minisink should be annexed to the County of Ulster.'

"This may have extended the borders of this old county in those days far down the valley of the Delaware into what is now New Jersey and covered the location of the mines.

"But what is meant by the mine, in this letter of Preston, lying north of the one on the Delaware and half way from there to Esopus? Was this the mine near Ellenville now called 'The Spanish Mine'? Were some Spaniards among those early Holland prospectors? We know there was one named Manuel Gonzales here as far back as the times of Dutch domination. There were others, both Spaniards and

Portugese, in the Esopus at that early day and, being of the nations who had exploited in Spanish America, they would naturally be drawn where minerals were reported. The tradition of an old Spanish mine at Ellenville, begun by Spanish prospectors, might have considerable justification could we but discover the facts. There is, however, nothing to show that anything but lead was ever found in the Shawangunk range." (Here ends "Olde Ulster".)

Mr. James Eldridge Quinlan, whose History of Sullivan County was published in 1873, tells us that the great trail from the Hudson to Minisink ran through Marbletown, Rochester, Wawarsing, Wurtsborough, Port Jervis and the Delaware nearly to the Water Gap.

In 1663 the Esopus Indians were humbled and a way opened to the heart of the Manassing or Minsi country, and soon after the treaty of peace the tide of emigration flowed through the valley of the Mamakating to Minisink, where the council fires of the great Lenape confederacy had glowed for many years. The Dutch treated the Indians well and had peace. The early days of Peenpack and Minisink are not recorded.

Gordon, in his history of New Jersey, says: "We may justly suppose, that the road between the colonies on the Hudson and Delaware was not wholly uninhabited", in 1658. He takes it for granted that the Minisink Road, which was one hundred miles long was the work of the Dutch, but Mr. Quinlan says: "And yet five years after this time (1658) there were not seventy-five able bodied male residents of Wild Wijk. It is not to be supposed that such a mere handful of men had hewn their way through a hundred miles of forest, infested by savages." Eager, in his History of Orange

County, expresses the belief that there were miners from Holland at work in the mine holes of Minisink and in the Mamakating Hollow, previous to 1664, and that the mining business closed in consequence of the surrender to the English in that year. Quinlan says: "If so, the country must have been explored by the Dutch and they would not have been compelled to employ as guides, in 1663, white females who had been prisoners with the Indians, and escaped; nor would they have resorted to Indians to pilot them through the woods to the forts and villages of the hostile clans, which were located within forty miles of Esopus."

"The error of Gordon and Eager is undoubtedly based on the interesting paper which was communicated by Samuel Preston in 1828 to Hazard's Register", (which is quoted by Mr. Brink.)

Pahaquarry is undoubtedly one of the mines mentioned by Lindstrom, the Swedish engineer, a knowledge of which, it is presumed, was imparted to the inhabitants of Esopus by the Minsi Indians, and led to the Minisink settlements above the Water Gap.

When in 1729-30 the Pennsylvanians questioned the right of the Dutch to their settlements, Quinlan says: "They (the Dutch) were shrewd enough to claim that their ancestors occupied the Minisink long before Penn purchased land of the Lenape; that in a forgotten age they had constructed a road one hundred miles through a wilderness country, to their possessions; worked mines, cultivated land, built substantial houses, and exercised undisputed control; that from generation to generation they had married there—reared their offspring there—grown gray there, and peacefully descended to the valley of death, where their flesh and bones had mouldered and returned to dust."

"When did the first settlers locate there? The Dupuis, as their name proves, were French Huguenots and the Huguenots did not come to this continent previous to 1686. The first comers, it is alleged, were miners from Holland, who worked in the Pahaquarry Mountain. Grant this, and still you do not concede that the territory was settled as soon as Gordon and Eager would have us believe; for in 1787, 'the old men were grandsons of the original settlers'. In the order of nature, this would have been the case, if the original white settlers had come as late as 1700. In one hundred and twenty-five years the grandsons would have been dead."

"In February, 1694, Capt. Arent Schuyler was ordered by Governor Fletcher to visit the Minisink country. He traveled through eastern New Jersey and reached the Neversink River above Port Jervis and thence passed to Minisink. He makes no allusion to white inhabitants of that region, although he speaks of traders and trappers, who had passed through it." We give his journal as quoted in Stickney's Minisink.

SCHUYLER'S JOURNAL.

"May it please your Excell:—

"In persuance to yr Excell: commands I have been in the Minissinck Country of which I have kept the following journal: viz.—

"1694 ye 3d of Feb.: I departed from New Yorke for East New Jersey and came that night att Bergentown where I hired two men and a guide.

"Ye 4th Sunday Morning. I went from Bergen and travilled about ten English miles beyond Haghkingsack to an Indian place called Peckwes.

"Ye 5th Monday. From Peckwes North and be West I went about thirty-two miles, snowing and rainy weather.

"Ye 6th Tuesday I continued my journey to Maggaghkamieck* and from thence to within half a days journey to the Minissinck.

"Ye 7th Wednesday. About Eleaven a clock I arrived at the Minissinck, and there I met with two of their Sachems and severall other Indians of whome I enquired after some news, if the French or their Indians had sent for them or been in ye Menissinck Country. Upon wch they answered that noe French nor any of the French Indians were nor had been in the Menissinck Country nor thereabouts and did promise yt if ye French should happen to come or yt they heard of it that they will forthwith send a mesinger and give yr Excellency notice thereof.

"Inquireing further after news they told me that six days agoe three Christians and two Shauwans (Shawnee) Indians who went about fifteen months agoe with Arnout Vielle into the Shauwans Country were passed by the Menissinck going for Albany to fetch powder for Arnout and his company; and further told them that sd Arnout intended to be there wth seaven hundred of ye said Shauwans Indians loaden with beaver and peltries att ye time ye Indian corn is about one foot high (which may be in the month of June).

---

* "Maghhackamack. This name was first applied to a tract of land in the lower Neversink valley. Subsequently that river was called the Maghhackamack. Ack or ach was the Lenape word for meadow, or land covered with grass. M'ack-h' ach-a-m'ach undoubtedly means a plurality of meadows."

"The Menissinck Sachems further sd that one of their Sachems and other of their Indians were gone to fetch beaver and peltries which they had hunted; and having heard no more of them are afraid ye Sinnegues (Senecas) have killed them for ye lucar of ye beaver or because ye Menissinck Indians have not been with ye Sinnegues as usual to pay their Dutty, and therefore desire that your excellency will be pleased to order yt ye Sinnegues may be told not to molest or hunt ye Menissincks they be willing to continue in amity with them.

"In the afternoon I departed from ye Menissincks; the 8th, 9th and 10th of Feb. I traveled and came att Bergen in ye morning about noone arrived att New Yorke.

"This is may it please your Excell. the humble report of your Excellency's most humble servt.

Arent Schuyler."

"In 1697, three years after Schuyler's expedition to the Minisink, a patent for lands in the valley was granted to him; also another for one thousand acres to the original settlers of Peenpack. There is no evidence that the Minisink country was settled previous to the year last named."

The original settlers of Mamakating were principally French Protestants who fled from their country on the revocation of the edict of Nantes. In 1697 they obtained a patent for twelve hundred acres in the Peenpack Valley at a place then called Wagaghkemek (Qu.: Maghhackamack).

"Subsequently, it is believed, a mine was opened and worked at a point north of Peenpack; but that from some cause it was abandoned."

Those who labored in the Shawangunk Mine in Mamakating cannot be styled settlers. When they abandoned the mine they abandoned the country, leaving no enduring trace behind them. After their exodus several years must have elapsed before the actual settlement of the valley began; long enough to cause the exact locality of the mine to be forgotten, otherwise it could be pointed out at this day.

"The first settler about 1700 was Don Manuel Gonsalus, a Spanish Puritan, who fled from Spain on account of persecution and married into a Dutch family at Rochester, Ulster County. He moved to Mamakating Hollow, built a log house and entertained those who carried wheat to the Kingston market", so says an early writer. Others do not agree, it being claimed that he was neither a nobleman nor a Puritan, and that while his name is mentioned in Kingston records as early as 1689, he did not come to Mamakating until after 1728, good reasons being given which are not copied here. It is not even certain that he was the original white settler, although such is the universal tradition.

The Old Mine Road terminated at the old copper mine in Pahaquarry a few miles above the Water Gap, and here we will leave theories and start with the main business of this book—a record of a tramp or tramps over the old and modern highway.

However there is one more document to be quoted, and then we are through with that sort of filling and can tend to the wild flowers and legends.

Count Nicholas von Zinzendorf came to this country in 1741 and founded the Moravian missions in Pennsylvania which were soon spread among the Indians in various directions. The Count in the course of his travels had occasion to cover the Old Mine Road and his journal referring to that part of his trip is given here, it being a "Narative of a Journey to Shecomeco, twenty miles southeast of Rhinebeck, N. Y., in August, 1742", and is taken from the Memorials of the Moravian Church.

MEMORIALS OF THE MORAVIAN CHURCH, Vol. 1, Page 47.

Narative of a Journey to Shecomeco, twenty miles southeast of Rhinebeck, N. Y., in August of 1742.

Count Zinzendorf, his daughter and Anton Seyffert left Nazareth, Pa., for Shecomeco. An old Indian trail led over the Blue Mountains through Tat's Gap into the Minisink; this led to Depue's ford over the Delaware River. Only such of the journal as covers the Count's trip over the Old Mine Road is given herewith:—

Aug. 11, 1742. "In the evening we reached the bank of the Delaware, and came to Mr. De Puis who is a large landholder and wealthy. While at his house he had some Indians arrested for robbing his orchard."

Aug. 12, 1742 (Sunday). "His son escorted us to the church and in course of conversation put a number of indifferent and idle questions on religious subjects. My inability to answer him gratified rather than chagrined me, and was. I thought, altogether an advantage on my side."

"We dismounted at the church, and were compelled to listen to two sermons, which wearied us.

"In the morning the heat had been overpowering. In order to avoid being drawn into religious controversy, I went into the woods and read Josephus. The Dominie came to me and annoyed me with questions and remarks. Although my curt manner provoked him, it served to bring him to reflection, and he sought to propitiate me afterwards by riding with us for several hours. He is the well known Caspar from Zurich, a well-meaning man, I must confess,—one of the so-called 'Convictionists', without much conviction, however, and yet efficient for good in his denomination."

The river is fordable at the head of De Pew's Island, a little above the house. The old homestead, thirty-eight miles below Port Jervis, is still in the family.

Aug. 13, 1742. "As we rode along, we were joined by a man who complained of the burden of his sins, and who inquired of me what to do to be saved. From his remarks, during the conversation, I failed to discover any solid ground, in his religious experience on which to erect an abiding superstructure."

"On passing a house, a female stepped out, spoke to us, and after the interchange of a few words, asked us to dismount, adding that her son, she knew, would be pleased to converse with us. We were unable to gratify her wish as we had purposed passing the Minnisinks, and through half of the widerness beyond, and there was a journey of thirty miles before us. When we reached the house that stands in the heart of it, night had already set in and it was dark as pitch."

Aug. 14, 1742. "Set out early in the morning; rode through the remainder of the wilderness, and reached Mombach and Marbletown. (Passed the night perhaps at the 'Jagd-house', half-way between Port Jervis and Kingston, or at Emanuel Pascal's.) We were much annoyed by the ill-natured questions that were put to us at a house at which we dismounted. Rode on through Hurley to Sopus. Here we met Sr. Anna and Christian Frohlich and his wife. I dispatched Christian to the Delaware to be with them at their festival, and retained Mary.

"In the afternoon we resumed our journey, crossed the North River, and halted for the night. The people here regarded us as Saints."

(Conrad Weisser, in his Journal to Onondaga, in August, 1750, gives the following stations and distances:—

Aug. 17, Came to Nazareth

Aug. 18, To Nicklas Depuy, in Smithfield, on Delaware ....39 miles

Aug. 19, To Henry Cortrecht at Menissing ....25 miles

Aug. 20, To Emanuel Pascal, "The Spaniard" ....35 miles

Aug. 21, To Kingstown (Sopus).......44 miles)

"On the 24th of August we set out on our return home."

Aug. 25. "Crossed the North River. Sopus being the Sodom of New York we resolved to pass through, and not spend Sunday within its borders. This prolonged our journey into the night and we barely succeeded in finding lodgings on the other side of Hurley."

Aug. 26 (Sunday). "I spent the whole day out of doors, and although I kept myself in the woods, I nevertheless got into difficulty. It was beyond my control to escape what the people here were determined to inflict on me. For in the evening, as Benigna (his daughter) was writing by candlelight in our lodgings, a Justice of the Peace came into the room and forbade us in the King's name. He then left in a storm of rage. Next morning at 5 o'clock (we were scarcely out of bed) a constable sent by him arrested me, Benigna, and Anton, and led us back to Hurley. Here were examined by the Justice in public; and without a proper hearing were convicted, and fined 18s. for Sabbath breaking. He then dismissed us with manifest regret that it was not in his power to impose a severer punishment. I really believe it would have afforded the people extreme pleasure to have seen us bound as scoffers of God and the King and taken down to New York. One of our Indians on being asked whether he wished to look on at the examination, rejoined saying: 'Why should I look on at such a malicious proceeding?' This answer vexed the bystanders."

Aug. 27. "Reached Minnisink.

Aug. 28. Came to the Delaware, across which we swam our horses."

"Deposition—Budingische Sammlung Part XV., No. 18?

"On the 26th of August, 1742, about 9 o'clock a. m., we, the undersigned, and three Mohican converts, sat down near a thicket, a short distance on the other side of Hurley. Soon after, our Brother von Thurnstein came to us out of the woods, and asked us whether we intended traveling further. We told him we thought of doing so. Hereupon, he earnestly advised us that it was Sunday, that the Presbyterians took offense at Sunday travel, and that on this account he had thought proper to make a halt. From regard to him we did as he bade us. He remained the greater part of the day in the woods (as was his custom), although it rained incessantly, and about candlelight returned to the house where we were lodging. Seeing his daughter Benigna seated at a table, he handed her a poem on the Indians he had composed a few days ago and asked her to copy it. She being unable to do it at once, he engaged in conversation, and spoke with much feeling of God's gracious dealings with the Economy at Halle, in the welfare of which institution he always took a lively interest."

"In the midst of the discourse a messenger entered the room and inquired whether any one of the company present had known the late Isaac Ysselstein of the Forks of Delaware. As Dominie von Thurnstein had had little acquaintance with him, and as he was always averse to engaging in any conversation with people on Sunday, he referred the inquirer to Dominie A. Seyffert. Dominie von Thurnstein now handed the poem to his daughter to copy and at the same time began to write in his memorandum."

"Although he expressly requested that no one should disturb him that day, several persons nevertheless entered the room and sat down. It was always left for him to conduct the religious discussions which usually followed the arrival of obtrusive visitors; but on the present occasion he confined himself to his writing, appearing disinclined to speak in the presence of the Indians, who all understood Low Dutch. Accordingly, he took no part in the conversation (there being some five or six of us, enough to answer all questions) until he was addressed personally. He had just finished his memoranda, and the Countess had completed the copying, when one of his visitors, who appeared to be the leader, remarked to him that he, the Dominie, seemed to be very industrious. 'Not at all', said the latter, adding, at the same time, that he was merely noting down a few thoughts. To this the man rejoined, saying that it was Sunday. Hereupon, Dominie von Thurnstein wishing to avoid useless controversy, observed that probably they differed in their religious views, but that, according to his belief, such writing as he had been engaged in was not unlawful on Sunday. 'The King', said the other, 'has ordered that Sunday be strictly kept in every particular, even in the face of the religious liberty which prevails in the land.' "

"This remark as well as the speaker's statement that he was a Justice of the Peace, and had spoken in the King's name, induced the Dominie to address a letter to the Governor in New York, in which he related what had happened."

"He took this step with the presumption, that in case the Justice were acting illegally in the premises, it would bring him to reflection; in case, however, his course was lawful, the Governor's endorsement of it would screen himself and his followers from slanderous reports. As often as this letter was presented to the Justice for delivery he persistently returned it with coarse invective; and early next morning, as we were about to resume our journey, a constable, sent by him, came to the house and arrested, with his tipstaff, first the Countess Benigna and next Dom. A. Seyffert. Dom. von Thurnstein accompanied them without compulsion, and hence the officer need not have touched him with his staff, and made a formal arrest. What else transpired, these deponents say not."

"We learned subsequently that the three were fined for Sabbath breaking, despite their protestations of innocence, that the Justice had alleged the Dominie's incivility to him on the previous night as the cause of his arrest and that he had returned the letter written to the Governor for the last time, in a passion and with threats."

"The bystanders on asking our Indians, after the arrest, whether they wished to be presented at the examination, the latter replied, that they took neither interest nor pleasure in such a malicious proceeding."

"Above deposition, although not made before a magistrate, we, the undersigned, eye witnesses of the occurrences therein stated, affirm to be strictly true. N. N. and N. N."

KINGSTON.

It will be noted that our amiable friend the Count has called Kingston "the Sodom of New York"; just why he did so is not plain, but I take credit to myself for a discovery made during the Fall of 1906, and that is that this same Sopus or Kingston is the site or immediate vicinity of the Garden of Eden, thus utterly refuting the slander that our missionary friend has placed on this beautiful city. The proof of this lies in the fact that Mother Eve is buried within its precincts as all may see who walk along the Fair Street side of the burial ground. Another interesting point developed is Adam's christian name, if early man can be said to have had a christian name. We all know that in the early days people were notoriously careless in regard to names, and while it is possible that the full name of our common ancestor is mentioned somewhere besides on the tombstone of his Eve, I have overlooked it, if such is the fact. It now seems that Adam was a Tenbroock and evidently a good Dutchman, and that accounts for another matter that has always been a puzzle, which is the evidently Dutch contour of the Prophets and other early Bible characters as illustrated on old blue tiles; in fact, I think I recall having seen on such a tile a portrait of either Adam or Noah waving the Dutch flag. It is astonishing how simple the most knotty questions become when sudden inspiration unlocks the door.

The City of Kingston celebrated the two hundred and fiftieth anniversary of its founding May 30th to June 1st, 1908.

On the 30th the inhabitants were so pestered with rain as to remind one of the same trouble the Dutch experienced two hundred and fifty years ago, when the floods prevented them for days from following after the Indians and their captives.

The remains of Governor George Clinton, which through the exertions of Mr. Benjamin M. Brink and Chaplain Randal Hoes had been brought from Washington, were reinterred in the Dutch churchyard in the afternoon, but the speechmaking by ex-Governor David B. Hill was adjourned to the court-house because of the storm. In the evening Major-General O. O. Howard, Judge Clearwater and Judge Hasbrouck delivered addresses.

Sunday, the 31st, was dedicated to memorial services in all the churches. At the Dutch Church Major-General Howard gave an interesting talk on Lincoln, rightly claiming that no patriotic celebration was complete without mention of that great patriot.

Dr. Van Slyke announced from the pulpit that on the following Sunday, June 7th, Chaplain Hoes would deliver an address recounting the attack on Wilt-Wick which opened the second Esopus war and read part of a letter from Domine Hermanus Blom, in which he craved permission from the Director General and the Honorable Council for an annual celebration by fasting and prayer to commemorate on each June 7th the event, and to give thanks for their preservation from the heathen.

June 1st was the grand day of the celebration. Here were parades and Indians and speeches, an attack on the stockade by the noble order of Red Men dressed as aborigines, while the night was illumined with fireworks.

I am reminded of a remark attributed to General Horace

Porter at the celebration of Kingston, October 17, 1893, to the effect that the Sons of the D. A. R. liked to place themselves on a plane below the Daughters of the A. R., partly from modesty, partly that we feel ourselves a little lower than the angels, and partly that we may obey the scriptural injunction which commands a man to set his affections on things that are above.

Kingston, with all its old stone houses, that are as attractive pictorially as they are from an historic and romantic point of view, offers wonderful possibilities for a fruitful imagination. There should be a dozen or more good ghost stories and romances waiting for some one to garb them becomingly for company. What a troop must cling around the Hoffman house, that stretches from the palisaded village to the days of the trolley, and how many romances have dated their opening chapters from the old ball room of the De Waall place.

It is no fault of the Dutch Church that its steeple has spells; certainly this beautiful, slender spire points the way to Heaven as both the architect and the builders intended, and yet there is a mysterious something, as one stands below and gazes to the diamonded shingles and small windows, that gives the imagination play.

It was well known some forty years ago that a spectral painter worked on this steeple of stormy nights, and then there is the hobgoblin's cap that was discovered one fine morning perched on its highest pinnacle—possibly it is some trace of one or other of these visitations, possibly of some long forgotten bewitchment; it is not for me to say. I can but report in good faith what has been told me, and leave the matter to the judgment of those better versed in such things.

Something like forty years ago it became necessary to paint this tall spire, but only one painter was found with nerves steady enough to undertake the work. This man, beginning at the base worked steadily upward until he reached the small windows, when he was suddenly stricken and died shortly after being helped to the ground.

There are those who claim that the workman died of painter's colic, but it is a singular and startling fact that he was not affected until he reached the level of the small windows mentioned above, and which are readily seen from the street. Now, such research as I have been able to make leads me to believe that that same hobgoblin, before referred to and about which we are to learn more shortly, had in some way been imprisoned among the rafters and there held by the holy spell and, lying in wait for the painter, had made faces at the man through the glass of a window and scared his breath away.

It must be admitted that this is largely theory, with little proof beyond the fact that the painter died.

Now comes the strange part of the tale: It seems that shortly after the death of the painter some citizen whose word was unimpeachable (some award the honor to Mr. Samuel Paulding, but there appears to be no positive means of identification) had revealed to him by a flash of lightning (or inspiration) one stormy night (or possibly it was through the bottom of a glass darkly—I am somewhat baffled here) the figure of a spectral painter high up on the steeple and hard at work.

The report spread quickly throughout the town and there was much excitement. While it was only given to certain elect brethren to see the spectre, there were yet enough to firmly establish the fact, as is evidenced by the current files of the local papers.

So far as can be ascertained, at this late date, this continued for but two or three years, and it is believed that the purpose of the spectre, whatever that may have been, having been accomplished, it repaired to some other job. The mystery has never been explained.

And now for the hobgoblin: In days of old, when sermons were long and church-goers were early risers, peculiar noises were commonly heard during the time of service, which were unkindly attributed to the throat action of certain worshippers, but which, in view of late developments, it now seems probable were ventriloquistic waves sent down from the steeple to bring unmerited shame on such good brothers as were wont to close their eyes for the purpose of more profound meditation. Be this as it was, these strange noises were heard regularly on Sunday mornings for many years, but are practically never heard to-day. I say heard on Sunday mornings; it is more than probable that had any been present during other days of the week similar or other noises might have been heard, but naturally no record could be kept of such—at least on earth.

It seems that some one of the old Domines had on a certain occasion made a journey to New York, and while returning on a Hudson River sloop with his good wife, a monstrous hobgoblin was suddenly discovered perched astride the bowsprit, much to the mental anguish of the lady and, in fact, of the entire crew. But our man of learning soon put the hideous creature to flight with an exorcism known only to himself and, strange to relate, the very next morning the cap of this same goblin was discovered hanging on the highest point of the

Domine's own church in Kingston and for many years thereafter these strange noises, already referred to, became manifest.

Presumably this goblin, in his violent efforts to recover the cap, became in some way incarcerated within the steeple and, being on holy ground, was deprived of his evil power; thus he was only able to vent his spite by such petty annoyances, until in an untoward moment his baleful influences were returned to him while the painter was at his work.

I understand that at Harvard has been established a chair of psychology, which undertakes to investigate well authenticated incidents of this sort and, so far as possible, explain them on scientific principles. It would be interesting to get this matter before the learned professors, and it is hoped that some one will use his influence to this end.

Here is a story taken from a book entitled "Rachel Dumont", and as most of my material is taken from the most reliable sources, I do not see why it is not permissible for me to give this tale just as it came to me:—

"Cæsar was an old colored butler in a Kingston family. He wore his hair braided on one side. The corresponding portion had been cut off by his nephew, Pompey, one day when the old man was asleep. Pompey's father caught him in the act, but old Cæsar always claimed 'it was dem rascally Britishers dat wuz tryin' to scalp him', and he was quite proud of his one-sided queue.

"Pompey said he cut the old man's hair off because 'Uncle Cæse put on mos' too much "grandiloquism" for a nigger, eben dough him is a butler'."

Before we get too far away from the church, I feel it my duty to lend a helping hand to the following facts, lest they perish by the way. In the good old days when sermons were not measured by time and the congregation was wont to follow "the comfortable Dutch custom of taking a nap", Doctor Gosman (the first minister called to preach in the English language—1808) was, on a certain Sunday morning, delivering a powerful sermon on the subject of faith, and used as an illustration the story of Thomas, called Didymus. In the gallery sat two brothers one of whom bore the christian name of Thomas, and he, having wandered to the land of dreams, hardly took in the full significance of the Domine's remarks; but, at last, becoming partially aroused by the frequent repetition of his name, as the Doctor in tones of thunder demanded, "Thomas, believest thou me?" finally answered back: "Wat begeert-u van my, Doctor Gosman?" His brother, greatly scandalized at the unseemly interruption, improved the situation vastly by vigorously shaking the drowsy man and saying in a loud voice: "Wees stil, man; wees stil! Hy spreekt niet van u; hy spreekt van Thomas Didymus."

On Crown Street, between John and North Front, stands the one-time "Kingston Coffee House", while over against it stands the Kingston Hotel, both of them dating back to an early period.

Mr. Schoonmaker tells how the landlords of both never drank at their own bars as a matter of principle; thus there was a certain nimble sixpence which made many excursions between the two hostelries as the proprietor of one or other desired to wet his whistle.

There is a pretty legend attached to the Kingston Hotel, which has Aaron Burr meet John Vanderlyn, the artist, here. The fact that the legend appears to clash with the facts to a small extent is no reason why we should not have it.

As a lawyer Burr traveled this circuit many times and was a well-known figure about the hotel. One day, on going to the stable for his horse, he discovered a young man sketching with charcoal on the great barn door and, struck with the lad's clever handling of his subject, spoke to him. Thus began a friendship which gave the lawyer an opportunity to help the poor artist to the education he most desired.

Schoonmaker's History of Kingston tells us that at the point where the road to West Hurley leaves North Front Street, northwest corner, stood the store of A. & A. Story, later of J. & J. Russell. On the south side of this store was an inlet communicating with a lane (Joy's Lane) leading southerly to Lucas Avenue. That inlet was originally the commencement of the old King's Highway to Hurley, Marbletown, etc. From that point, taking a somewhat circuitous course, it struck into the present road a short distance west of the old Winne house. The change to the present road was made in 1813.

On the south side of this "intake" and at the corner of the lane stood the stone mansion of Nicholas Bogardus. General George H. Sharpe has recorded how Nicholas spent the later years of his life in protecting a fine plum orchard back of his dwelling from certain predatory boys who were fond of plums. His chief weapons were a stout cane and a series of well selected Dutch oaths with which the young rascals were bombarded. The boys, however, appear to have worn oathproof armor, and were quite content could they but keep out of reach of the cane, which, it is to be presumed, was not always the case, and returned to the charge the moment the old gentleman retired from the field. Thus the latter lived an active, if not peaceful, life and through much exercise a healthy and vigorous old age, while his happy command of language was the subject of many congratulations.

While in this vicinity it is interesting to note the origin of Lucas Avenue, which has its name from the fact that it was the starting point of the "Neversink Turnpike Road", in which Judge Lucas Elmendorf of Kingston was the moving spirit. This was organized July 3, 1807, and ran through Hurley, Marbletown, Rochester and Wawarsing. It nearly paralleled the free highway and finally formed a junction with it at Accord. The scheme did not pay, so in 1817 the name of the company was changed to "The President and Directors of the First Great Southwestern Turnpike Road Company", but even such a grand name failed to insure a success and the president and directors were soon looking for another job.

On Lucas Avenue, a step beyond Joy's Lane, still stands one of the old "jail limits" stones, a reminiscence of the times when folks who could not pay for what they ate and wore were committed to the county jail until they could, a highly satisfactory arrangement, no doubt, to the creditor and taxpayer, for then the poor debtor was cared for and none need worry lest he go hungry. In due time some one discovered that the joke was on the taxpayers, and "jail limits" were established and the debtor was discharged "on the limits", he agreeing not to go beyond the stones which were set up on the main thoroughfares one mile from the jail in all directions, and to report to the jail every day, Sundays and holidays excepted. One undesirable feature to the debtor of this arrangement was the fact that he must secure a bondsman who would pledge twice the amount of the debt, and if the debtor overstepped the bounds by ever so little or so short a time and was caught at it the bondsman must pay.

There is a legend of that old gray stone house erected by Colonel Wessel Ten Broeck in 1676, and now known as the Senate House, which is too beautiful to change, and is given just as it comes to me:—

In some time far remote there lived in this gray mansion a wealthy Dutchman, as staunch to the principles of the government of his ancestors as he was rich. Alone with him lived his beautiful young daughter, whom he kept secluded and guarded from the small world about them.

One night there came a rap at the heavy oaken door, and as the hour was late the father answered the call, swinging wide the upper half-door and asking who sought admittance. The answer came in English: He was a stranger on his way from New Amsterdam to Van Rensselaerwyck and sought shelter for himself and horse. The youth was admitted, though the good man hesitated, being ever suspicious of the English, and neither speaking nor understanding their language any too well. The fine physique, the noble face and apparent wealth and refinement of the guest demanded and won the respect of the host.

The Englishman was no more conversant with the Dutch language than was the burgher fluent in the use of English. Conversation was difficult and they soon abandoned any attempt to talk. The stranger's eyes wandered about the fire and candle lighted circle; the shadows hid the maiden, but the light fell upon the shining body of a rare old violin on the high mantle. The stranger grasped it eagerly, and gently saying, "Here is a common language—I will speak to you", he raised the violin to his shoulder and produced such rare harmony as was never before heard in Wiltwyck.

On and on he played, lost in a spell of his own weaving.

The old man's head bowed, his pipe was forgotten in reveries of his home land; the maiden moved out from the dusk as one drawn by an unseen force and stood in the light with shining eyes, glowing cheeks, parted lips and hands clasped before her.

The youth now saw her for the first time, an enchanting picture of enraptured and radiant beauty. He realized the power of the music; he felt the charm of her sweet, young being. On and on he played—for her—now softly as the sighing of the winds in the Summer woods; now the martial strains that tell of tramping feet, of conflict and of victory. The long pipe of the father fell to the hearth before the bright logs, and the reveries gave place to dreams of heavy slumber. The violin was put aside and the young people understood the lovelight kindled in each other's eyes.

When the old man awoke he found his daughter in the gallant's arms. In anger he sent her from the room and in grim silence conducted the other offender to his chamber. His wrath was in no wise calmed in the morning and he hastened the departure of his visitor. The lover was not in haste to leave his lady, and haunted the plain near the old stone mansion for days, meeting her secretly, but the music they loved betrayed them.

The father ordered the maiden to be locked in her room and the despairing lover went sadly on his journey. For days the girl in sweet melancholy visited the places she and the stranger had frequented. She fondled the violin as a thing which had been voice to their mutual love.

Her father found her thus engaged kneeling on the hearth in the firelight. His anger rose at this rebellion to his wishes and he seized the instrument and roughly dismissed her. She went to her room but never left it again. For little more than a fortnight she lingered between life and death and faded away, unheedful of her father's entreaty for forgiveness, but seeking one last favor. She requested that the dear old violin be sealed in the side of the ancient Dutch chimney before which she had first heard her lost lover play, and this request the contrite father gladly granted.

The loyal spirits of the lovers still meet on the hearth before the chimney of the "Old Senate House", and only true, loving souls, disciples of the mystic truth in life, hear the sweet melody of the English lover's unseen violin.

—[Edith M. Elting.

Mrs. J. L. Preston tells a singular incident which occurred to her aunt when the latter was a small girl. A schoolmate being very ill, she was sent by her mother to inquire after the sick one, and returned shortly with the information that it had not been necessary to make inquiry, as she had seen her young companion on the walk in front of the house, that she looked about as usual and smiled on her. Later in the day it was learned that the child had died just about the time her little friend had reported having seen her.

When this occurred the "aunt" was but eight or ten years of age, and too young to appreciate the strangeness of the situation, and she is described in after life as of an unusually phlegmatic and unemotional temperament. It is therefore impossible that there could have been any make-believe about the matter.

On Frog Alley which, before the Esopus Creek was bridged, led to the ford, stands an old Bogardus home. Some time prior to the Revolution and down to about 1818 this house was occupied by one Roe, the silversmith of Kingston, who turned out some very good work. An apprentice who learned his trade here under Roe, Vallette by name, also had something of a reputation in the art.

In those days there were only about eight hundred silversmiths in the entire country; each made his own designs, was an artist and a man of more or less distinction.

Here is a true witch story from Saugerties, the principal actor in which is still living:—

Some forty years ago a young boy in Saugerties who was musically inclined much desired an organ, and about this time he was taken with violent tremblings and twitchings which greatly alarmed his parents, who finally called in the witch doctor, and he, after studying the case with great care, announced it a most serious one, the only remedy for which was that the boy be passed a certain number of times through the belly of a freshly killed and disemboweled beef, the carcass to be thereafter hung in a well.

This was done, but without the desired effect. My notion is that the carcass in the well was hung wrong end up, and the doctor was again called in. By this time the boy appears to have made the doctor understand what ailed him and the good man announced that he believed music might effect a cure, so the lad secured his organ and immediately thereafter was he made whole.

The Kingston Hotel in Hine's day.

The east end of the Senate House in Hurley (*above*) and the well (*below*). Both photographs are from Hine's personal copy of *The Old Mine Road*.

HURLEY.

"Loop, jongens—loop;	Hasten, children—hasten;
De Rooje komme;	The Red coats come;
Span de wagen	Hitch up the wagon
Voor de paerde	Behind the horses
En vy na Hurley toe."	And run toward Hurley.

One fine Spring morning I left Kingston on the Old Mine Road, bound for the mine holes on the Delaware. This was the year of the daisy; not for a long time have they been so beautiful or abundant. The farmer hereabouts calls them bulls-eyes and welcomes them with a mowing machine where he can, for they spoil the grass, but they make a wonderfully attractive foreground for pasture and mountain. As I walked a sound came that startled me, even though I could see by the open mouth and stretched neck that it emanated from a mooly-cow, so like was it to a fog horn down on the Massachusetts coast that I have heard many a time—even the soughing in of old mooly's breath helped along the illusion, for it was so like unto the gentle lapping of the wavelets on a pebbly shore. Being on pleasure bent, I stopped and listened for a moment, closing my eyes and going back in memory to mornings when I have stood at an upper window and looked out on nothing and listened to the calls from unseen vessels in the harbor or the sudden hammering of a horse's hoofs on the wharf and the as sudden silence as the horse came to earth again, as startling in its way as a sudden crash.

The milestones up here measure the shortest miles that I

have ever walked, though they agree fairly well with the distances as laid down on the maps; the three miles from Kingston to Hurley are a notable example of this brevity of the miles, the surroundings are so unceasingly attractive. A glance down Spook Hollow failed to show Mr. Spook, though he may have been there for all that. My eyes are stigmatic, which may have something to do with the uncertainty of his whereness, for I must look straight ahead through glasses, and my notion is that a ghost is best seen out of the corner of one's eye. Last year, when up this way, our spook was carrying his head in his hands like a Jack-o'-lantern, but what the style of wearing it is for this year I was not able to learn, for it is to be presumed that when one has a detachable head there would be little variations in the manner of carrying it just, as I understand, the method of carrying a cane changes from season to season.

The spook hole is because witches and spooks were wont to gather at the bottom of this gully, which lies near Gus Elmendorf's. The only case of a spook being actually seen there that I have been able to run down is that of a gentleman of Hurley who, returning late one night from Kingston, found that his horse absolutely refused to pass the spot, no matter how he applied the lash. Finally he dismounted and when on a level with his intelligent beast saw a spook, in shape like a man, leaning against the fence, and being fully persuaded of the reasonableness of his horse's fright, and solely in order to relieve the animal's mind he promptly turned and galloped back, making his way home by another route.

Once around the corner into Hurley Street, I soon found the open door, and entered thereat to find that the friends had rather been expecting me to make an early start and drop in for breakfast. My! how fine the old Senate House did look, all dressed up. Its colors are two-thirds patriotic and one-third Irish—red, white and green—though the Doctor insists his father was an Englishman. Now that the old place is getting used to its good clothes and conveniences it must wonder sometimes how it ever got along with any sort of comfort at all in the old days. It turns out that the east room with all its shelves is not to be the kitchen at all, but a library, and back of it the snuggest little writing room that ever was: Hawthorne described it when picturing the Old Manse:—

"In the rear of the house, the most delightful little nook of a study that ever offered its snug seclusion to a scholar. * * * The study had three windows (ours has only one, but never mind) set with little, old-fashioned panes of glass, * * * The two on the western side looked, or rather peeped, between the willow branches down into the orchard, with glimpses of the river through the trees. The third facing northward, commanded a broader view of the river at a spot where its hitherto obscure waters gleam forth into the light of history." The description is not as perfect a fit as I thought it was going to be, but somehow it made me think of the Doctor's "den" when, in an hour's idle reading, I ran across it some time ago.

The Doctor finds that old deeds of Hurley lots describe the property as bordering on the "King's Highway", but the Rochester town records speak of our Old Mine Road as the "King's Highway" and the Hurley deeds may not necessarily mean that this was the great north-and-south "King's Highway" which Mr. Brink believes held its course between here and the Hudson—through Green Kill and so east of the Binnewater Lakes—but rather that which led into the western wilds.

The orchard lot back of the Senate House has not been

plowed since 1860, until this year, when it is being put into potatoes, and now many arrow points and spear heads are turned up. An Iroquois bowl was recently found in a bank nearby.

It has always been claimed that the Council of Safety removed from the "Senate House" because, no matter how warm the debate, the language used immediately froze and fell to the floor. This kept the speaker on the jump lest his toes be smashed by the heavy words and took the mind of the orator from what he was saying to such an extent that no business could be transacted. The Doctor says that "sentimentally it is pleasing to look upon it so", but that the action of the Council of Safety indicates that the weather had nothing to do with the removal.

The Council desired the Governor to disband it and call a meeting of the Legislature. The Governor, however, objected that his duties would not allow him to come so far north as Hurley, but suggested that if a meeting were held at Poughkeepsie, he would act according to their wishes, as he could arrange to come there and at the same time look after the fortifications intrusted to him by Washington. The Doctor suggests that we see the Proceedings of Council of Safety for November 27, 1777, but as it is all written out here plain enough, I see no reason why we should go further:—

"I Cadwallader Colden Esq. Do solemnly Promise unto Charles DeWitt & Gouverneur Morris, a Committee of the Council of Safety of the State of New York by the Councill afors'd appointed to mark out and Settle the Limits and Restrictions by which I Shall be Confin'd, upon my Enlargement from the fleet prison, that I will forthwith repair to the House of Cap'n Van Deusen, at Hurley, and will not go more than two miles from said House without Permission of his Excellency George Clinton Esq. the gov'r of the said state, That so long as I shall Continue Confined as aforesaid, I will not by writing word or deed Do or be Privy to any acct matter or thing whatsoever to Promote the Interest Jurisdiction Claim or Authority of the King or Parliament of Great Britain in or over any Part of North America, And I pray God to help me as I shall keep this my Solemn Oath & Engagement. C. C.

Sworn at Kingston in the County of Ulster
this 3rd day of Sep'b 1777
Gouv'r Morris
Ch. D. Witt."

The Doctor thinks he has laid the Senate House ghost with so simple a contrivance as a wooden door latch. The unseen hand on the latch of the "Antiquarium" door has caused many a cool draught of Winter air to come between the Doctor and his wife, and he has fled to evils that he knows not of by removing the old iron latch which sufficed his predecessors and substituting therefor a contrivance made of wood, and this does seem to work.

Just what are the properties of a wooden latch that make it proof against the unseeable, or what kind of a charm the Doctor worked into this particular latch, I know not. The Doctor has made a study of these things and his knowledge is past belief, but what fears me is the thought that the Senate House ghost may attempt some other mode of keeping the household informed of its presence and that the last state of the old house may be worse than the first.

Not every one can have a ghost about his home; it is a sign of respectability that no money can buy, and the Doctor had best beware. We know that the building is much above a hundred and fifty years of age, and it is reasonable to suppose that the ghost may think it has some rights that a wooden latch has no business to interfere with.

The old hotel in Hurley is no more. On March 18, 1909, about 5 in the morning the village was aroused with the cry of fire, but the discovery was made too late and soon nothing but the crumbling stone walls remained of this historic building.

The hotel was erected in 1716.

The early courts were held here.

It was the rallying point for patriotic meetings during Revolutionary times.

General-Governor George Clinton had his headquarters here when he attempted to aid Kingston in October, 1777.

The members of the Council of Safety resided here when the Council met in the Van Dusen house.

When General Washington passed through Hurley on his way to Kingston, November 16, 1782, the President of the village delivered from the safe shelter of the hotel porch the address of welcome, while the distinguished (I had almost said extinguished) visitor sat his horse bareheaded in the rain, which example his staff were under the necessity of following, though they no doubt, like the gentleman mentioned in Psalms, blessed with their mouth while they cursed inwardly.

We soon started out for a pleasant morning with the Daisies and other wild things that lurk in the nooks and corners of Hurley' suburbs, and followed a footpath across the fields to the western hills and along the sinuous roadway at their feet until Vollicher Falls came into view—merely a thread of water that leaps into the cosiest little basin, and after stopping to get breath trickles away in a little brook that our Irish setter nearly swallowed whole. There may be times when more water adds to the excitement, but nothing could well add to the peaceful delight of the spot. Continuing on we came to the stone road that carries the westing Kingstonians back into the hills. Then we marched back again and a bit later found ourselves moving south over this same road, catching glimpses of distant Mohonk and of the valley of the "Dug Road", interspersed with gleaming little brooks, old stone houses, clumps of Meadow Rue and other floral fantasies until we came to the Judge Elting house, the object of our afternoon journey. This was "The Depot at Marbletown" established by Governor George Clinton in May, 1779. As early as October, 1777, says "Olde Ulster", the Governor had determined to establish a storehouse and magazine at Marbletown to deposit military supplies, not too far from the river and near enough to the frontiers to be available in their defense, but while goods were distributed about the neighborhood they were not collected under guard until after the attack on Fantine Kill showed the necessity for such action, when the house of Andries De Witt was selected for the depot and a guard placed at night.

We found the lady of the house very willing to show us its interesting points. The Doctor is much like Aladdin's lamp in these parts, all one has to do is to rub him—the right way, of course; though any old way seems to be the right way—and lo the doors open and the hearts of the people with them and we are shown the treasures of the past with a gladness that makes them doubly attractive. We also found the most inquisitive lot of calves around the outer walls that ever were blessed with a propensity to investigate. They crowded around the cameras, felt in our pockets and stepped on our feet with all the abandon of youth; in fact, one had to draw the attention of our curious friends while the other took the picture. It was quite evident that they had not been nurtured in the fear of man.

Hurley appears to have been stocked with real witches from a very early date, but as in all such matters, innocent persons will occasionally be suspected. The Hurleyites, however, used no such crude methods as did the good and gracious Pilgrim Fathers—here was no cutting off of ears, nor is there record that the ducking-stool was used to settle the vexed question. The method employed with Betsey Conway is illustrative and, while quite as efficacious, left no unpleasant after effects so far as could be observed.

Betsey lived in a log hut near the watering trough on the Wynkoop property, other side of the creek, and was strongly suspected of being a witch. One day while calling at the home of Cornelius Hotaling, a daughter of the house placed salt under her chair. Now a true witch under such circumstances is helpless, and when Betsey arose when the time came to go and without difficulty left the house she should have cleared her fair fame of the imputation, but folks will talk.

Another and instantly effective way of settling the matter was to stick a pin in the bottom of a chair in which the suspected person sat. Under such circumstances the witch is held fast and wholly unable to move, while the innocent person proves the fact promptly and to the great gladness of the assembled company. The writer can testify that he has never to his knowledge seen a witch sit on a pin.

Sometimes unsuspected witches would be accidentally discovered as when an uncle of a local luminary, while hunting, discovered a large deer which he shot at without result, except that the animal, no doubt having the Biblical injunction in mind, turned the other side toward the hunter who, then suspecting where the trouble lay, found a bit of silver in his pocket with which he loaded his gun, and this time hit the game, only to lame it, however, when immediately a person in the neighborhood went lame, thereby proving that she was a dear, I suppose.

There was a time when I used to go hunting myself, and in those day was notorious for shooting at bewitched deer. It would have helped my sporting reputation immensely had I only known where the trouble lay and the simple remedy therefor, but that has nothing to do with the subject-matter in hand.

On another occasion a neighbor, though a good shot, missed several times while attempting to bring down a hawk, until some one told him to try a silver bullet, and with this he killed the bird instantly. About this time an old woman who was believed to be a witch, died, thus proving that she had taken possession of the hawk and that the silver bullet killed her as well as the bird. Sounds almost like a case of absent treatment, does it not?

It was a common trick of the witches to cast a spell over the guns of hunters, and no one thought of venturing out for game without at least one silver bullet in his pouch.

But these meddlesome and altogether no-account persons caused trouble indoors as well as out. Aunt Jane Elmendorf was so hindered in her churning on one occasion that the butter would not come, no matter how much of a dashed time it had, until she was finally compelled to put a horseshoe on the bottom of the churn, whereupon, the charm broken, the butter promptly came.

Doctor Jacob Brink, of Katrine, was the witch doctor for all this region. He and his sons were also called "finger doctors" from their success in curing diseases by the laying on of hands. I can recall with painful distinctness how they used to try that on me when I was a small boy, and how they firmly believed that the result was beneficial, though the process never in the least had my approval.

On account of the machinations of the witches and of the obstacles placed in his way, no ordinary person was able to summon a witch doctor—only a seventh son could overcome the difficulties. Such a one was Jacob Bonesteel, of West Hurley, but even he at times met with vast opposition. On one occasion he became mixed up with fences in most inextricable fashion, was caught and held by trees and generally had a most bothersome experience. The writer believes that he recalls having read in a history of witches and marvels, entitled "The Thousand and One Nights", how witches were sometimes confined in bottles, and escaping on the removal of the cork caused great confusion and entanglement with fence posts and things, causing said posts to place themselves directly in the path of the bewitched person and to deliberately collide with him, but we must get back to Jacob Bonesteel; my tendency appears to be to wander.

Jacob finally reached the doctor who, coming out, wrote a few lines on a bit of paper, waved his hands, and the traveling thereafter was so easy as to become positively monotonous.

A cardinal point to remember, once the witch doctor had been sent for, was to allow no one in the room, as the witch could and would enter with a visitor and, once inside, could negative any good the doctor might attempt. Of course she could have been kept out by a broom placed across the doorway, but no one seems to have thought of that. In the particular case in hand a child was the victim, and while Jacob was dodging the fences, trees and other sirens of the highway, a neighbor called and in this way the witch was let in, who thereupon remarked "Auntie has come to see you", and when the witch doctor came he discovered the situation and told the relatives that he could do nothing beyond punishing the witch, which he proceeded to do to the great satisfaction of the family by cutting the child's shirt with his whip, explaining that just so many times as he hit the shirt did the witch receive strokes upon her back. It has not been learned whether the child was at the time within the shirt or not.

A sister of an uncle of a true believer was cured of a fever sore on her leg by a "finger doctor", who rubbed the spot gently and at the same time repeated an incantation, which caused the sore to entirely disappear. We have finger doctors even to-day, but I believe they are now called osteopaths.

Doctor Brink was the only one who could kill a witch without the use of a silver bullet, though he could delegate this power to others. Otherwise the witches "dried up and blowed away"—such was the fate of an old witch that once lived in Beaverkill.

The mother of our friend Jacob Bonesteel was once sitting quietly in the house when on a sudden she found she could not move; then entered a witch who had been bothering the boys at hog killing outside and said to her the magic words "come on", and the old lady moved without difficulty. No Christian Scientist could have made a better job of it. Every one knows what an obstinate thing a hog is, but not every one knows how doubly-dyed is its obstinacy when bewitched. The boys were killing hogs, but they finally came to one who, like Achilles, had been made invulnerable at all points but one, and that one was hot water—it is well to remember that no witch can stand hot water—and after exhausting all other methods, they were compelled to resort to scalding, before which no hog, bewitched or otherwise, can stand. It is a well known fact, established by the traditions of the fathers, that it does not do to slaughter a hog in the wane of the moon, for then the fairies take all the fat for their lamps, while the farmer gets all the lean. Sounds rather like Mother Goose, but facts are stubborn things.

There is yet living a woman who can bear testimony to the disconcerting effects of being bewitched. When a girl she lived with Domine Blauvelt, of West Hurley, and for a time when she was in the house, the good man experienced great trouble in his household. Everything was mixed up. His gold spectacles were found in the stove, as was a silver thimble;

Note—To cure warts. Take green bean leaves; place on the afflicted part and then lay the leaves under a stone and as they rot the wart will disappear; if it does not disappear that is evidence that the leaves or something were (or was) too green. Or, take a piece of pork and place it on the wart; then throw same over the left shoulder, using the left hand for the purpose, closing the left eye and placing the tongue in the left cheek during the operation. When the pork rots the wart will disappear. If in this case the wart does not disappear that is a sign that some dog found the pork.

An old Hurley cure for fits. Take 9 drops of blood from the right ear of a cat and administer to the patient.

In order to bewitch a person the witch must borrow 3 separate articles from the to-be-bewitched.

A witch track placed on the bottom of a churn was a 5 pointed star; if this was of no effect a red-hot horseshoe was tried.

the sugar bowl was discovered in the woodbox, handfuls of dust in the milk pans, and such a general mixedness was there that the Domine was at his wits' end. Finally suspicion fell on the maid, who was watched and caught in the act, when she admitted that her grandmother had put a spell on her. She was then hurried to the witch doctor and cured, and to-day is living the orderly life of a respectable married woman with an abundance of small children.

The following is one of those simple, old-time receipts that were so efficient in the days of our grandfathers, and it seems to me worth preserving. The chest from which it has lately been taken had not been opened for years and this was with other papers dating back seventy-five to one hundred and fifty years. The informant of the gentleman who forwarded this and whose intelligence led him to at once see the value of the document states that in his early days such a cure, or at least a similar one, was frequently used. The paper is quoted literally:—

"A Cure for the Spavin:: last friday of the last quarter of the moon, take the head of the horse to the east; begin on the left side of the horse and take a piece of every foot, of the frog, then goe around the horse to were you begin and take a bit of hair by the shoulder end by the hip and goe a round to weare you begin then take a bit of hair of the curle of head and put it in a paper together, the frog first then the hair and make a 3 quarter fold and put the paper in it and plug it shut in and sweet apple tree to the east side of the tree befour sun rise whithout speaking a word."

A certain Hurleyite is the possessor of a stone that is locally regarded as an Indian effort at carving an Indian head with a feather head-dress, which was found on the flats at the foot of the graveyard many years ago by John L. Elmendorf.

Inquiry of the Peabody Museum in Boston elicits the statement that it is a "slick" stone, used by the Indians in working down thongs and also in preparing various fibres for strings and sinew thread.

The Smithsonian Institution responds to the same question that it is of that class known as "whetstones", and while it may have been used for dressing thongs, it was more probably employed in grinding down other objects of stone. The stone is possibly a half-inch thick, is three and eleven-sixteenth inches long by two and one-half inches at the widest point.

Advertisement from the Ulster County Gazette, July 10, 1802:—

"Notice is hereby given

"That the remaining seats in the Church of Hurley will be sold at public vendue on Saturday the tenth day of July. Those persons who have subscribed with an interest to purchase seats will be pleased to take particular notice that if they neglect to purchase at this time, they will be debarred hereafter, as the seats not sold at this vendue will be disposed of in another manner.

"All those who are in arrears by Subscription, or for Seats purchased in said church will please to settle the same without delay, with Mr. Egbert Roosa.

"The vendue to begin at two o'clock P. M. on said day and due attendance given by the Consistory.

"Hurley, June 31, 1802."

The good book tells us that there is no new thing under the sun, and Hurley helps to prove the rule. In those parts of the country which run open street cars in Summer there has developed a species of biped known as the "end-seat hog", which we believe is generally regarded as a modern development due to changed environment. But it seems that Hurley was the better part of a hundred years ahead of the rest of the country, as witness the following official document of the Hurley Church—that church which formerly stood over against the Senate House:—

Among the "Miscellaneous Acts of the Consistory" is—

"An Act of the Consistory of the Congregation of Hurley For the better Regulating the Seats of the Church of Said place.

"Whereas some difficulties have arisen with respect to the Rights of Different Individuals who have Purchased Seats upon the same bench in said Church, with respect to the extent and distinction of Their Rights.

"Consistory wishing therefore to do away all misunderstanding upon this Subject, and to restore & maintain Perfect harmony among the Proprietors of said Seats do declare that the first principle upon Which the Seats were sold and the Deeds given was that there was never to be Any distinction of the Seats of Individuals upon their respective Benches and that Such Individuals were Proprietors in Common of Said Benches Possessing undivided rights Corresponding in exact proportion to the Number of Seats they purchased And that Said proprietors had no Right Conveyd. to them by virtue of Said Deeds Ever to Choose any particular part of any Bench or pew Purchased as above.

"The Consistory therefore Ordain as a Standing regulation of this Church as it respects Said Benches or Pews and the Rights of Individuals thereto, that the Person or Persons who

Shall for the purpose of Divine Worship Enter into any of the Said Pews or Benches first after Comming to said Church Shall as soon as the other Proprietors or any of them may come for the purpose of Divine Worship to the door or doors of any of Said Pews or Benches, Immediately move up on the Bench So as to give room for the other Proprietors So that their shall be no passing by one another or crowding or justling in Said Seats which is always indecent in the house of God and very offensive to the true worthiness of the most High.

"This Resolution however Shall not be Considered repugnant to any agreement that now or may hereafter Exist among individuals Provided Such Agreement is consistent with order and Decency————By order of the Consistory.

Hurley (signed) Thomas G Smith Preses
26 Decembr. 1806."

When the British burned Kingston there was naturally a good deal of fear of the "Red Coats" among those who loved peace. The following two or three stories are taken from a little book entitled "Rachel Dumont", published in 1890:—

A field of rye had just been cut in Hurley, but when it was known that Kingston was burning the workmen dropped their tools and left the half raked grain to care for itself. Thus a rake lay with the teeth up, on which a young farmer, crossing the field, happened to step, when the handle promptly flew up and hit him a hard and sudden blow on the nose, whereupon he immediately threw up his hands and yelled "Hurrah for King George".

The day following the arrival of the American soldiers in Hurley the usual "noon gun" was fired. Pompey, a slave in one of the refugee families, although he had done much boasting as to what would happen to the Britishers if he ran foul of them, hearing this gun, rushed into the farmhouse, exclaiming:—

"Lord Massy: dem Britishers am comin' agin! Good Mr. Lordie, spare dis poor fambly, an' de niggers, too. Ole Grannie, she's ole an' sick, an' wan's to die; so take her fust, if yer mus' heab some un. An dad he can go wid her fer comp'ny. Pompey has too many wimmen an' childers to take care ob; he can't be spar'd jes' yet."

Then he hid in a great barrel of potatoes, where he was found some hours later by his father, who came for potatoes, and who exclaimed:—

"Lor's a massy, wot's yer doin' in dis tater bar'l? Has yer been about suffin' orful wicked ag'in and feard de good Lord'l cotch yer? Come out, yer nigger, an don't spile all dem new taters."

"Oh, daddie, I done thort dem Red Coats was comin' and I's so afeared dey take yer an ole Grannie dat I come in de cella' to fire at dem truegh de trap door. Am dey come?" responded the valiant Pompey.

"No, no, chile—de good Lor'll tak car of poor ole Daddie and Grannie; yer's a brave boy, Pompey, to 'fend yer 'lations, an s'all hab a big piece of water mellin fer yer dinner fer not fergettin' the old folks, Pompey, some niggers is jes' like white folks an' jes' looks out fer der own sef's. But yer is a waryer an' no mistake."

In an old account book wheat is spelled as follows: Wett, weat, wheate, weate, whitt, whaet, wheat, witt and weett. Those were the good old days when every man was his own dictionary. We are not one bit happier to-day, if we are more precise over minor mattters. It was a favorite saying of my father that it was a poor word that could not be spelled more than one way, which leads me to think that wheat must be a multi-millionaire. And in this same class can Hurley itself be placed for old records give it to us as Hurly, Horli, horrely, Hurrely, Horly and Horley.

Here follows an advertisement from the Ulster County Gazette of October 26, 1799, the reason for which is not altogether evident to me, unless the advertiser proposed to sell his horses to unsophisticated New York:—

ULSTER COUNTY GAZETTE. October 26, 1799.
(Advertisement)
"Wanted to purchase
a few fat Dutch
Horses

If they are TWENTY and shew for SEVEN they will answer. None need apply after ten days from date hereof.

Hurley, October 18, 1799. (Signed) Eli Sears."

So far back that I do not know just when it was, Hurley boasted one of the few militia companies in uniform, and because of the color of the uniform, and for no other reason whatever, this company was known as the "Hurley Greens"—they were not vegetables, mind you, but men of war.

Now, during the anti-rent war in a neighboring county, the Hurley Greens were ordered out for police duty, but the members did not like to be used in such a cause and it took a summons from the Sheriff to get them into line. Finally some of them went, and on arrival at the seat of war were placed on sentry duty the first night.

The password for that night was "moon". During the hours of darkness one of our valiant friends was greatly perturbed by a person approaching through the bushes, and they do say his teeth rattled some; but still the stranger approached without offering to give the countersign until he of Hurley could stand it no longer, and blurted out: "Say 'moon', damn you, or I'll shoot", whereupon the approaching stranger kindly said "moon" and all was peace.

A certain neighbor who lives out on the Marbletown road is a devout Christian, but somewhat practical withal. During a long continued drought the Domine happened to remark to this good brother that he thought it advisable to pray for rain, to which the deacon responded: "That's all right, Domine; but you'd better wait for the new moon."

A few specimens of English from an old Hurley account book:—

Anno Domini, 1756.	£ s d
1 peare Shouse Meade for your wife.........	00. 6.0
1 peare Shouse petch for your Neger Jough...	00. 3.0
2 deays Riding with horses and wagen au Do..	00.18.0
3 bearlears of Syder at the press at 8s........	1. 4.0
1 peare of Shouse Meade for your Neger Whinch Gin	00. 6.0

Another account, 1757:—	£ s d
2 Schiples of Weet at 4s. per Sch'pl	00 8.0
to 1-6 an Agys (eggs)	0. 1.6
4 Ells of humspon for apetecot	0.12.0
Credit	
by making a Chist that is a Coffin for our Whinch	00. 4.0

Another account.	£ s d
to Maind My teecatel	00. 1.6
fixing bagnet to a gone	
by Making a Cock to my Gone	00. 9.0
2 hug Seds	1. 4.0
1775 to 4 broms I geir corn for to the ingines...	00. 2.0

West Hurley once boasted of a citizen who was on the town and proposed to stay there. He became such a thorn in the side of those who were compelled to care for him and his that many attempts were made to bring him to a sense of his position, but all without effect. Finally his neighbors concluded to try a scare, and announced to the old fellow that as he was entirely useless on this earth they were intending to bury him on a certain day, to which he readily assented.

The threat, not having the hoped-for effect, his friends next procured a pine coffin, proceeded to the house and informed lazy-bones that they had come to attend his funeral. Even this failed to stimulate to activity, and they then placed the old chap in the coffin and proceeded. Well, they had not counted on any such ready acquiescence to the proceedings, and were much perplexed as to the final outcome and, in the hope that something might develop which would arouse their burden to a sense of his shortcomings, they stopped each passing neighbor and explained in a loud tone and with many words what was being done.

Each moment matters became more and more desperate, until finally one was stopped who, on hearing the story, said "Put him down boys, I have a couple bushels of corn that he can have and that ought to be a start toward something better". Up to this point the corpse-to-be had shown no interest in the proceedings, but now he raised up and inquired if the corn was shelled, to find that it was not, whereupon he lay back and said "go on boys, it ain't no use".

MARBLETOWN, STONE RIDGE AND ACCORD.

After a night spent under the roof of the Senate House, I was fitted out with a pocket full of lunch and the Doctor and the "dorg" went along as far as the next (the fourth) milestone. And now that the milestone is past and my companion has turned back, I am inclined to tell on him. The Doctor has a wife who is a great Bible student, nor does she mind getting one on her husband when an opening occurs, thus she not infrequently quotes holy writ at him and at least one such quotation is, it seems to me, worth recording for the benefit of those who do not search the scriptures daily. It is to be found in 2 Chronicles, XVI., 12-13, and reads as follows:

"And Asa, in the thirty and ninth year of his reign, was diseased in his feet, until his disease was exceeding great; yet in his disease he sought not to the Lord, but to the physicians. And Asa slept with his fathers."

Before we can possibly get away from the village one sees a dab of green paint that proved to be one of the interesting old Hurley houses—or was it blue paint, my chief recollection is that it was some kind of a blot on the landscape. This is where the first Masonic lodge for this locality was established and that is why we stop and look at it. Asking for a drink I was sent to the spring which boils out of the bank of the Esopus at the rate of a barrel a minute, it was everything that a spring should be; refreshing both to the eye and throat and having been told where to find the cocoanut shell cup among the roots of an old tree, I helped myself.

"Yes, fountain of Bandusia,
  Posterity shall know
The cooling brooks that from thy nooks
  Singing and dancing go."

Sink holes in a limestone country are by no means uncommon. Opposite the second milestone out of Kingston is one in a field. Another opposite the fourth milestone was recently discovered by a cow of roving disposition, whereupon our bovine explorer hoisted her tail over the spot, much as explorers of old planted the King's standard and, like an old knight, she bravely gave her life to the cause, for when the farmer saw the signal she had raised he found his cow wedged head down in the rocks and as dead as Cæsar, though not quite so dusty.

The day was something warm, the air full of the smell of growing things. A delightful breeze kept me company down the road, but unfortunately it was traveling my way and at about my gait, and I only knew of the fact because the trees were waving to it a welcome. To my way of thinking a blow in the face had been better than to have so softly kept me company.

The old Pawling house soon came along and I stepped over into Marbletown. Then there was the Esopus where it bumps into the highway, a tent among the alders on the other side and a canoe drawn up on the shore suggested camping and fishing and doing nothing, and most anything else that a tent and a canoe and a pleasant little river might suggest.

Here was the sixth milestone, and about three-quarters of a mile beyond, or just before the seventh milestone is reached, in the village of Marbletown, stands a famous old tree, on land owned by Louis Bevier. This is within a few feet of the north fence in the bend of the old road; a new cut-off here leaves it still further afield.

This is an ancient landmark, so ancient that it is said to have been a noted mark on the old Indian trail from the Esopus to the country of the Delawares. A great, solid chestnut tree that is estimated to be over five hundred years of age. A singular feature is a white elm which at the base is entirely surrounded by the spreading trunk of the chestnut. About eighteen inches from the ground the elm springs from the trunk of the older tree as a branch might, there being no indication of a split in the chestnut trunk. Five feet from the ground the elm and chestnut, in close apposition, measure twenty-two feet three inches in circumference, the elm being probably thirty inches in circumference.

The great age and size of the tree, its historic interest and the remarkable singularity of the growth combine to make this of more than passing interest.

Many years ago Marbletown was visited by a great wind which demolished the church. All the congregation turned out at the rebuilding, even Domine Davis lending a hand in the good work.

While thus engaged a certain man from Hurley came to view the operations, and remarked in a casual sort of way that it seemed to him significant that the church of God should thus be destroyed in Marbletown while no harm had come to that in Hurley. To this the Domine retorted, "Well, you know that there are some people that even God Almighty will have nothing to do with".

Now we have the house of the widow Davis, tavern and

town hall along about 1680 or so. Then the road climbs a hill from which one can look down on and wave a farewell to the Esopus, for we separate here, while across the level bottom lands, green with the coming crops, and beyond the tops of nearby hills is spread a grand panorama of the Catskills—a multitude of peaks. The buzz of a wandering bee become dainty through an excess of riches helped to emphasize the fact that the day was warm.

In the midst of the wonderful picture is the Summer home of Mrs. L. E. Schoonmaker, who owns the old Depue house in Accord that we are coming to shortly.

Now it is Stone Ridge, in the early days known as "Butterfields", where are the Hardenburg house, a one-night stand of General Washington, and the Tack house, in which court was held after the burning of Kingston by the British.

At a very early date Aart Pietersen Tack came to this country and was one of the pioneer settlers of Wiltwick. Here a son Cornelius was born, but some time later the father appears to have made a move in the wrong direction, and with the aid of the courts his wife became Tackless. The lady then married a Van Etten and henceforth has nothing to do with our story. Cornelius in due time had a son Jacobus, and he a son Cornelius, and he again a son Johannes, and the house that Tack built is supposed to have been erected by this Johannes some time before the Revolution.

A great-grandson of Johannes tells me that when he was a boy the overhead floor beams showed incisions of bayonets and marks of gun muzzles; that the attic, which was then one long room, was known as the "Lodge Room" because the Masons held their meetings here.

The house was run as an inn by Johannes and by his widow,

Sarah, after him, she being succeeded by their son John, who continued the business until nearly 1830. There is a tradition that on the occasion of Washington's visit at the Wynkoop house in 1783 the members of his staff stopped at the Tack house, as the place was a tavern and directly opposite to the Wynkoop house, I should say that we might accept the tradition without straining our swallow to any extent. At Hurley December 9, 1777, an order was given to apprehend certain men seen at Jacks Tavern in Stoneridge carrying out leather to Bethlehem, Pa.

The road works over a ridge and loses the Catskills, but Shawangunk looms large ahead and Mohonk keeps to the front as though the Smileys knew how to run the landscape as well as they do a hotel; in fact Mohonk has been sticking up in the middle of things off and on ever since yesterday and continues to do so for the better part of another twenty-four hours, as I discovered to-morrow.

Shawangunk was originally the name of a specific place from which it has been extended to cover the mountain Chauwanghungh, Chawangon, Chauwangung, Showangunck. The name has been applied to the mountain and stream since the second Esopus war. It may mean "at, or on, the side hill". The Indian palisaded village called "New Fort", and later Shawongunk Fort was on the brow of a tract of table land on the east bank of the Shawangunk Kill.

Mohonk may mean "a great tree". The name was originally applied to a spot at or near the foot of the hill, and later spread to the hill itself. The correct Indian name was probably Maggeanapogh, meaning "a great rock". These, as are most of my other explanations of Indian names, are taken from "Indian Geographical Names", by Mr. E. M. Ruttenber.

Finally the road forks beyond Stone Ridge, where the 12-mile stone shows the way. That at the left leads straight down to Kyserike on the other side of the Rondout.

A good many years ago, when Jay Gould had yet his fortune to make, was a country surveyor in Ulster County and was doing most any job that promised bread and butter, he was well known up and down these roads. In later life when he was accounted a rich man, one who knew his history accused him of still owing a shoemaker in Kyserike a small amount for repairing his shoes in the early days, but Gould responded that this could not be so, as he always repaired his own shoes in those days.

Kyserike is modern, and never was on the Old Mine Road anyway, so we will keep to the straight road and worry down to the Rondout at Accord. Here stands the old Depue house on a brook that the map tells us is Peters Kill, but which is locally known as Monesauing Creek.

The old Depue house is nearly two hundred years old, built by Moses, who came to Rochester a boy in 1662. He bought the property of the Indians, and it has never since been out of the family, Katie Depue being the last to actually occupy the old home; she died January 31, 1884. The above is from Mrs. L. E. Schoonmaker, nee Depue, who turned to the old family Bible for names and dates.

The old house never saw any very exciting times, so far as is known. The only Indian incident is related of one Joseph Depue, whose mother understood the Indian language and, when she heard an Indian, who had been around looking for her son, vow that he would kill him, the old lady sent a colored boy to warn the young man and it is handed down in the family that Joseph saw the Indian first.

The house of the widow Davis, Marbletown. Photo from Hine's collection.

The Tack house, Stone Ridge, with a ten-mile marker in the foreground. Photo from Hine's collection.

Rondout is generally taken to have come from a small fort or redoubt built at its mouth. Mr. Ruttenber writes that after the erection of a stockaded redoubt here the Dutch called the place Rondhout, which may mean "standing timber".

John James Schoonmaker, better known as "John Jim", is one of those mortals who likes to know who his grandmother was, and incidentally has picked up much local information, having been town clerk these many years, and he has studied the old records which, thanks to his good care, have been put in savable condition. The first Schoonmaker was Hendrick Jochemse S., a native of Hamburg, Germany, who settled in Albany before 1655. He kept an inn and was a man of means as he is reputed to have loaned money to Governor Stuyvesant. Was among those who came to Esopus in 1659 to assist the whites in repelling the advances of the reds, was attracted by the richness of the lands and settled permanently in the region. Naturally I found my way to the Schoonmaker house and Mr. S. opened the safe and took out the old records for my inspection. They are beautifully written and very easy reading, at least so are the earliest of the writings, the first entry beginning:—

> "To all christian people to whome this present writing shall or may come Coll. Henry Beekman, Capt. Jochem Schoonmaker & Mosys Du Puy the present trustees of all the land of the town of Rochester in County of Ulster send greeting. Whereas there is a general pattent obtained for all of the land of sd town of Rochester", etc., etc.
>
> "this 22d of Sept. 1703."

The two volumes bring the records down to the time of the D. & H. Canal, 1828, or thereabout.

One of the curiosities of the old books is the fact that nowhere is the old-style letter s used, but invariably the modern form. At first our road is mentioned as the "Queen's highway", but by 1718 it is the "King's Highway".

The recording of these deeds was in many cases for people who had been settled in the town for some time, for in September, 1703, mention is made of a "corne" mill on Mombaccus (old spelling) Kill or "Rivelett".

The temporary character of boundary marks is illustrated over and over again, as "Beginning at a great Black oak tree standing in a dry gully by the Rondout Kill or River side * * * and runs in woods by a line of marked trees * * * along the highway to a marked white oak tree and so from thence to a marked 'Nutton' tree standing on the east side of Munasanink brook", etc., and again "Beginning at a white oak tree marked Standing on the northside of the east Sproute of a Certain Runn of water called the Mudder Kill", or we have "a small white oak tree marked with three notches and a cross over them".

Where Mattacahonts Kill flows into Mombaccus Kill is now Mill Hook. An early owner of the water power here was a Quick, possibly an ancestor of the famous Tom; the bounds of his property are frequently mentioned in descriptions of adjoining grants.

The first Hoornbeecks mentioned are Lodowyck or Lodewick or Loodwyck, and Anthony; one or other owned the "corne" mill at the high "ffalls" of the Mombaccus, which is mentioned in September, 1703, and one or other is presumed to have built the old stone house, which stands south of the road about two miles west of the Accord bridge.

"The Creek called Hoonck" is mentioned; possibly this is

where we get Hunk or Honk Falls from. Johannis G. Hardenberg was town clerk, 1704-5. His writing, while it looks smooth at first glance, is one of the most difficult to read in the book. In some cases the ink used has, where a heavy stroke is made, eaten the paper completely away. Mosys Du Puy's name suffers at the hands of various town clerks, who transcribe it without giving much heed to the facts. In one document it is Mosys du puy—on the very next page we have it as Moses Dupuy, and so on.

The question of hogs and sheep was a live one, and many are the rules made for their government. Fences were fifty-two inches high, English measure, and from that "hight" to the ground sufficient to turn cattle.

Mombacus means in Dutch a "mask", a grotesque face, and the story is that early settlers found a rude face carved on a sycamore tree near the junction of the Mombacus and Rondout Kills, which is supposed to have recorded some victory for the local Indians. The town records of one hundred and fifty years ago refer to the bridge over the stream as "the great or high bridge across the Mombaccus Creek" as though it was the eighth wonder of the world. The government map ignores the old name and calls our Silent Face "Rochester Creek".

Accord remembers a former citizen named Bell, who was apparently cracked in the making. Some twenty or twenty-five years ago he told how, having seen a bolt from heaven drop into the creek, he next morning investigated and discovered a sword sticking up out of the water, much as King Arthur found that "fair sword" Excalibur given to him by the Lady of the Lake, who in the history of le Mort D'Arthur, is called a "damosel", which spelling bringeth me immediately back to our friend Mr. Bell and twenty or twenty-five years ago. The sword was a two-handed affair and covered with rust, the removal of which disclosed strange figures of men and animals, much after the fashion of prehistoric scratchings. Bell evidently knew enough about metals to know that there was no alloy of iron and silver which would furnish the hardness and other qualities of his find and claimed that his celestial sword contained a large proportion of silver, an impossibility in any but a celestial sword. He then called in a chemist, in order to have a bit of the metal assayed and secure a certificate, should silver be found therein, wherewith he could confound and silence all doubters. In the chemist's presence he filed off an innocent looking piece from the guard which was sent to the laboratory to be put in the crucible, but the assayer, fearing that if an accident happened to the crucible the charge would be lost, cut the cube in two, expecting to make a duplicate assay. On cutting the piece, however, he found a small bit of silver which had been inserted through a hole bored in the iron, the external evidence of the job having been concealed with a coating of rust and gum. No certificate was issued and the celestial sword went the way of the discovered fake.

Mr. Bell appears to have never wearied in well doing others, for we next hear of him as lodging at Dannemora because of some little irregularity in connection with a deed to property that insisted on belonging to those who purchased it.

If Bell had lived along the Esopus one might understand where he caught his bent, for that stream will get out of bed most any stormy night and steal land from nearby farmers. It is told how one man down in Hurley lost three acres last year, and the curious thing about it is that while every one knows who the thief is no attempt whatever is made to apprehend him, and so, grown bold by long immunity, the creek, like history, repeats itself when the mood takes it.

As we progress on our way, we begin to hear of Indian foray and massacre, but the region immediately around Accord, or Rochester as it was in the old days, appears to have been a sort of doldrums both during the French and Indian and the Revolutionary wars, for no serious trouble of that nature is recorded for these parts.

The highway through Accord keeps in such close touch with the creek that it seems in danger at times of falling in, and no doubt would, were it not for the trees which so kindly keep watch and ward along the steep bank, but the creek is too crooked for any well ordered road to long keep in touch with, and we soon went a little way off. The old burial ground here, which probably dates back to 1703, offers a remarkable curiosity in a tombstone more than half buried in the trunk of a monarch of the forest; the tree has literally grown from one side to beyond the centre of the stone, so that less than half of the inscription can be read.

PINE BUSH, KERHONKSON AND WAWARSING.

The Dutchmen seem almost from the very first to have built their houses of stone, and consequently there are many still standing that date back to the first settlement. As we approach Pinebush, some two miles beyond the Accord bridge, a long, low building is seen well back from and south of the road, known as the Morris Myers house. This is the old Hoornbeek place which it is claimed was a "fort" in the French and Indian war times. Here was dwelling at the time of my call Miss Esther Atkinson, who has charge of the village school, and who takes a very keen interest in matters historic. She immediately took me in charge for a trip around the house, and was even willing to frame herself in the old Dutch double door for the benefit of the camera, a very small Myers doing his or her share by standing on tip-toe to see over the top of the closed lower half what the camera was up to, and being caught in the act.

This house, so my guide said, was attacked but once, the Indians approaching from the creek. In approaching thus over the fields they had no cover, and it is supposed did so on the theory that the defenders were away; fortunately, however, they were not only at home, but had been warned and provided such an unexpectedly hearty welcome that some of the visitors were quite overcome while still others shyly ran away. The house was not loopholed, but is said to have had the same dormer windows in the roof that are there to-day, and it was from these that the defenders fired on the approaching foe. Such windows would seem to indicate that the house was of more than ordinary consequence, as the attic story was generally used for storage and only lighted from the ends, but the glass in the present windows has the iridescence that only comes with age and bears out the theory that they have been there from the beginning.

This neighborhood is known as Pinebush, and in all probability the attack on the Hoornbeek house mentioned above was that of September 5th, 1778, when three houses were burned, two men killed and one taken prisoner.

This July day was better for corn than for folks on foot and the dust was worse than the sunshine. Up above it early began to look like showers, and by 1 o'clock the hill folk were getting theirs, but the storm went off in the direction of Kingston, where was to be seen much thunder and lightning. By this time I had climbed the long hill out of Accord, had viewed the Hoornbeek house and had dropped down to the creek level to lunch on ice cream and snaps at Kerhonkson, an Indian appellation the meaning of which does not seem to be known.

It seems that John Kettle was murdered by the Indians near the east end of the Kerhonkson bridge, and for many years thereafter his ghost haunted the bridge on dark nights. There is an old gentleman still living in this neighborhood who bears testimony to the fact that in the early days several persons had seen Kettle's ghost on the bridge—there can be no doubt but that it was the ghost of Kettle and no other, because those who saw the vision said it was. It must have been most inconvenient to meet a ghost midway of a covered bridge, and particularly when one could not be quite sure whether it was a ghost or a bit of surreptitious moonshine come in by way of a knothole, at least not sure of it until he got to the telling of it at the village store.

About a mile further on and to be seen both from the old roadway which sticks close by the creek and from the new which parallels it a bit further back, stands the old Hardenbergh house "where the records were stored". When New York was certain of capture by the British the records of the colonial government were moved up the river to Kingston and "Olde Ulster" tells us that on October 12th, 1777, four days before the latter was burned by the invaders, the records were loaded on ten wagons and taken back into the country along our Old Mine Road and committed to the "care of Hendricus Hoornbeek, Comfort Sands and Johannis G. Hardenbergh, Esq., according to a Resolve of the Council of Safety for Said State of New York, and deposited in a room in the Hardenbergh dwelling, believed to be the north room, which is the one at the right of the illustration. The finish of the room, even in its present state of decay, indicates a building of superior construction.

The capstone of the outer door bears the date of construction, "1762", and the monograms of the family in which are letters for each syllable of the name Hardenbergh. Under the eaves on either side are three portholes. So long as the records were here the house was at all times under guard.

"Hurley, December 17, 1777. Resolved that the State Records at Nepenagh be kept there under guard."

Northwest of the house on the summit of Turkey Hill are the graves of the family, the horizontal stone which marks the grave of the old patriot being inscribed:—

"In Memory of
Johannis G. Hardenberg
who departed this life
April 10th 1812
Aged 80 Years 9 Mos. 17 days."

The house where John Stall now lives was in early days the John Kettle home. The head of the house was caught outside by the Indians and scalped, but his son with John G. Hardenbergh and other neighbors who answered the call for help, successfully defended the place from further molestation.

Wawarsing is another Indian name the meaning of which is not known, but again Mr. Ruttenber comes to the rescue with a suggestion that it may be from an Indian word meaning "at a place where the stream bends". The village is one long street, well lined with houses for a distance of a mile and a half; as we get well within the eastern end of the cluster an evidently old building on the left cannot help but attract attention. The immediate locality here is known as Sockanisank, or Socconessing, as it is more modernly pronounced. This is the old Indian name of the neighborhood and, according to Mr. Isaiah Rose, means waterhole, swamp, marsh, and any one with half an eye can see why it was applied.

This old building, says Mr. David Crist, who is the local historian of these parts, represents three periods—1616, and two additions made in 1716 and 1783. The earlier date is something of a surprise, as it antedates the settling of Kingston by thirty-seven years. Mr. Crist calls this the Depue house, but does not know who built it. At the time of the Fantine Kill massacre, the Indians came this way, when the only occupants of the building are said by Mr. Crist to have been an old man and a boy of sixteen. The elder, of course, counseled caution and the saving of their fire until the enemy was close upon them, but the boy, with the impatience of youth, could not forbear taking a crack at a chief who was some distance in advance of the other Indians. Fortunately his aim was accurate and the chief immediately became a good Indian. Being a chief his companions picked up the body and retired to an Indian burial ground near the bank of the creek. On their return they evidently thought the house too well guarded for attack and passed it by.

This oldest building in Wawarsing is claimed to be the birthplace of Governor De Witt Clinton. The birthplaces of this celebrated man are so numerous as to call for some comment, and as this is the first that we come to in our travels, it looks as though the comment was about due. But we do not wish to be understood as criticising the gentleman for it was really a matter entirely beyond his control.

De Witt Clinton's father lived in Little Britain, not far from Newburgh, and some years ago, when the question of his birthplace was a matter of some acrimony, one Edward M. MacGraw of Plymouth, Wis., wrote to the Independent Republican in January, 1874, claiming that the event occurred in the home of General James Clinton, his father, because his (MacGraw's) mother told him so. Mr. MacGraw was born and reared in Little Britain, and his parents knew the Clintons well and used to point out the residence as the birthplace of De Witt C., and that was satisfactory proof for him.

Then there is the old darkey who claimed to have been a servant of De Witt Clinton, who in 1881 was living in Honesdale, Pa., and who was reported in a Port Jervis paper as having said "the Governor was born in Little Britain, Orange Co., and no mistake", and that settled it in the minds of those who favor Little Britain.

New Windsor comes next on the list and here the building is still standing in which he was born, and that is proof enough for most folks down that way, who can see no use in arguing over a fact. A letter written to the Goshen Democrat in 1836 said that by common report of the neighborhood, confirmed by the Clinton family, De Witt Clinton was born in New Windsor.

And now we come to Wawarsing. Just across the highway from "the oldest house" lives Mr. Benjamin Bruyn Russell, whose mother, Elsie De Witt, was an own cousin of De Witt Clinton's mother, and consequently he has it very straight from one who knew all the circumstances that De Witt Clinton was born in this old house.

The fourth spot where this event happened is just across the Rondout from Napanoch, on the left as we traverse our Old Mine Road. The Napanochers point to the building, a low frame that looks too modern, and which is probably much like Mark Twain's jack-knife, though the cellar hole may be the same. The Hon. Thomas E. Benedict, who lives across the way, believes this to be the place, because he has talked with members of the De Witt family and all their traditions point to it. In 1873 and in 1881 the Ellenville Journal championed this as the Mecca toward which the devout should bend their steps.

In Port Clinton is to be found the fifth and last place, so far as my discoveries go: Here, in February, 1769, in the sharp angle of the road at the top of the hill, stood the stone house or fort of Jacob R. De Witt, brother of Mrs. James Clinton, and here was De Witt C. also born. This is rather in the nature of a bare statement of fact. I have heard no arguments in its favor, except that the other fellows have not proved their cases, and here was a near relative at whose house the lady might easily have been staying when the event occurred.

The story told to account for the fact that De Witt Clinton was born away from home is the same in each instance. General James and his lady had been visiting at the home of a relative, and just as they were about to return a great snow storm descended on the valley, which prohibited comfortable travel for months and detained the visitors long beyond the contemplated time.

It looks to me as though the Governor was born again about four times, and while this is rather rough on his mother, I hardly see how we can help it or how the facts can be accounted for in any other way; it is simply one of the penalties of greatness.

As we pass down the road toward the west we come to a lane on the left leading to Indian Hill, in the near corner of which, now a vacant lot, once stood the old stone church of Wawarsing. The date of erection is unknown, but "Olde Ulster" says that a church had been here long enough to be described in 1742 as the "Old Meeting House". At the time of the last Indian raid down this valley, August 12, 1781, the savages entered the church and amused themselves by throwing their tomahawks at the panels of the pulpit, leaving a number of gashes which were never repaired. Two of the more venturesome of the whites attempted to shoot some of the invaders as they stood in the church door, but one gun missed fire and one gunner missed aim and they were compelled to run for it without having done any damage. The church stood until 1843, when it burned.

Keeping down the lane and through a farm gate we see on the right the John C. Hoornbeck house, formerly the dwelling of a Vernoy. At the moment of attack only Mrs. Vernoy and her baby were about the place; she in the barn and the child in its cradle in the house. Two of the enemy entered the house, Shanks Ben, a noted Indian, and a Tory, who was one of the party. The woman, knowing it was certain death to show herself, was compelled to remain where she could, unseen herself, see into the open door of the house. Thus she saw the savage go to the cradle with raised tomahawk to strike, when the babe smiled in his face and he could not bring himself to kill it; but not so the representative of civilization, who without compunction dashed out the innocent life. Even a babe's scalp had a money value in those days, for the English appear to have deliberately put a price on scalps.

Toward the close of the war a British detachment was captured on its way to Canada and among its baggage were found literally bales of scalps, representing 340 men, 88 women, 193 boys, many girls, but number not given, 29 unborn infants and 122 mixed, old and young of both sexes.

Continuing along the lane we stop at the next bend where across the fields can be seen the notch which cradles the Vernoy Kill. In the immediate foreground is the site of the stockaded stone fort used during the Indian troubles.

The "Narratives of Massacres and Depredations on the Frontier in Wawasink" mentions the fact that one Philip Hine and another were acting as scouts at this time and were captured by the Indians.

Naturally this is of interest to a member of the family, but who this Philip Hine was is something yet to be learned. As the men of Massachusetts and Connecticut frequently worked their way over to this frontier, it seems probable that he, as are the rest of us, was a descendant of Thomas Hine, who is believed to have come over with the Rev. John Davenport, who landed in Boston June 26, 1637. Within two years Thomas Hine removed to Milford, Conn., of which town he was one of the founders. But the genealogy of the family makes no mention of any Philip.

If the Mohawks had lived up to their traditions they would have done better by Philip Hine than tie him up to a tree in the woods and leave him for three days without food or drink, for the Connecticut histories tell how the Mohawks, coming over to Milford on a maraud, about 1645-50, were surprised and defeated by the Milford Indians, who tied one of their captives to a stake planted in the salt meadows and there left him to be eaten by the mosquitoes.

"An Englishman named Hine, who found the poor wretch in this deplorable condition, shocked at this barbarous mode of torture, cut the thongs from his limbs and set him at liberty. He then invited him to his house, gave him food, and helped him to escape. This kind act was never forgotten by the Mohawks. They treated the English of Milford ever after with marked civility and did many kind and friendly acts that testified their gratitude toward their deliverer and his family."

Another says:—

"For this simple act of humanity Hine was much endeared to the tribe of the rescued Indian, who believed that the Great Spirit would always watch over and protect the good White Face and his posterity."

Possibly the Indians neglected to ask Philip his name.

Passing through another gate, the lane finally leads down to the Vernoy Kill just before it enters Rondout Creek, and here we come on the site where tradition says stood the council house of the Esopus Indians and other tribes of the Hudson and the Delaware.

In a deed of this land dated in 1699, the following appears: "excepting a certaine part or parcell which is called Anckerops land running to a Creek where the great wigwam now stands", etc. This is the only record of the council house that Mr. Brink has been able to find.

Under the shadow of the mountain, when the sun is in the west, once lived Benny Depew, in a little old stone house. When the canal had a better circulation than is now the case the place was known as Port Ben. Now it is merely the railroad station for Wawarsing.

Benny was in many respects a second edition of everybody's friend, Rip Van Winkle, his strong point being a love for that kind of work which counts least in dollars and cents—hunting and fishing and the telling of his adventures to an admiring group of neighbors.

But Benny is not our story, he is merely an incident, or an instrument through which the following facts have been preserved:—

Old Ninety-Nine, an Indian chief, said to be the last surviving remnant of the Ninety-Ninth Tribe, and a great hunter and trapper, found in Benny the reincarnated spirit of the brave, whose scorn of the hoe was only equalled by his love of the chase. And to him the proud chief confided the great secret that had been handed down from chief to chief and must die with him.

Whispering that he had an unheard of wonder to show, that not even his own brother could get from him, the chief invited the trapper to go on a trip with him, and one day both were quietly swallowed up in the dense forest that then clothed the sides of old Shawangunk.

Climbing among the rocks and ravines of this mountain is no work for a tenderfoot, but both men were equally seasoned, for Benny could follow wherever the Indian led. Up, up they clambered, over rocks and fallen trees until they finally came to a dry channel that during the spring freshets was swept by the melted snow from the heights above.

Here the white man allowed himself to be blindfolded and, after following the water trail for about an hour, the Indian removed the bandage and our explorer found himself at the foot of a high ledge of rocks, but so surrounded by trees that he was unable to locate the spot in the deep gloom of the primeval woods.

As Benny looked about him he saw nothing very wonderful. There were, perhaps, a hundred such ledges on the mountain, but the muscular old giant led to a great boulder which he pushed one side and exposed to view the mouth of a cavern, into whose blackness Benny could only blink in amaze.

Old silent face, lighting a bit of candle, beckoned the now frightened woodsman to follow. These rocks and gullies were full of gnomes and goblins and such a step seemed like bearding the lion in his den. But the Indian strode on and the white man was bound to follow, so with trembling fingers he clasped the sleeve of his guide and they pressed forward. Almost immediately the passage opened into a great vaulted chamber, when it seemed to Benny as though his fairy godmother must have waived her wand, for beneath his feet were the richest and most costly of rugs and oriental carpets, so thick and soft as to deaden entirely the sound of their heavy tramp, which but a moment before had echoed and re-echoed from the rocky walls. While on every side were waving arras of costly tapestry with beautiful vases and rare articles from China and the Ind. standing and lying in profusion, pictures so life-like that the subjects seemed about to start forward to greet the guests or landscapes where the trees appeared to wave in the wind and the brooks to sparkle in the sun.

But the "chief do-over", as our elegant friend Mr. Dooley would say, was an immense chest, over which the Indian swayed his lighted candle and through whose sparkling contents his long, claw fingers ran, for it was filled to the brim with all manner of gold and precious jewels, diamonds, rubies and sapphires that glittered and sparkled under the yellow rays of the candle until the whole room seemed to be alight with the flash of their splendor.

Finally the chief awoke Benny from his trance with the announcement that they must return whence they came, and after reaching daylight the great boulder was rolled back and the Indian looked to see that their feet left no sign. Then bandaging Benny's eyes once more, they returned down the mountain.

Ninety-Nine never offered to conduct Benny to the cave again, and so long as the Indian lived his companion feared to search for the place, but the red-skin finally went on his last hunt, and as time passed and he did not return, the desire for the treasure overcame Benny's fear of goblin vengeance, and he finally set out to seek the cave for himself.

He was a good woodsman and easily found the spot at which his eyes had been covered, and he then proceeded to follow the dry run, but soon it began to branch and branch again, and he was lost in a tangle of dry water courses such as he never before knew existed, and it took him some time to realize that the guardians of the treasure had spread this network all about to confuse and confound him, but when it was once clear to him what the trouble was he hastened home and never again ventured on the quest, for many a man who has excited the ire of these guardians of the mountain's secrets had gone on a hunt never to return. And, what is more, their bodies are never found, but on stormy nights when the trees sway and bend to the blast the groans and cries of the lost are plainly heard and it is well known that they had been imprisoned among the branches and trunks of the trees, which took delight in crushing, crushing, crushing until, as the storm increased the tortures of the captives, they groaned aloud in their agony. Every man who knows the woods has often heard these terrifying sounds as the wind has swept the tree tops.

As Benny became old and garrulous the story finally came out bit by bit, but none were found bold enough to undertake the exploration for long years. But in these days when there are many who profess to have no faith in witches and hobgoblins (a very dangerous and distressing condition, surely,) one will occasionally be found to take up the search.

One such industrious gentleman was reported by the Ellenville Journal some dozen or fifteen years ago as having found the cave. The tapestries and carpets had, of course, long before rotted to dust and many rocks had fallen from the cavern's roof and buried the treasure deep, but our adventurous friend was intending to pack a backload of good blasting powder to the cave with which to uncover the treasure for his own benefit and that of his heirs and assigns forever.

But nothing appears ever to have been heard from the adventurer again and whether he pulled the hole in after him and could not get out, or whether the goblins put him to sleep will never be known.

It is possible that some day some one in league with the Devil may be allowed to sign his soul away for the treasure, but probably none but he and his friends will ever know it.

Just how all this treasure, which was loot of the white man, not the Indian, got into this out-of-the-way place, no attempt is made to explain, but there is an old legend which tells how Captain Kidd attempted to steal the share of a partner, who staked him for a certain cruise, by running the two returned vessels heavily laden with spoil up the Hudson. The contents of one vessel is said to have been carried back into the Catskills and hidden—may not this be it?—the other being taken further up the river.

The oldest house in Wawarsing at the time Hine was making his journey. It is one of five houses in which De Witt Clinton was alleged to have been born.

NAPANOCH AND ELLENVILLE.

If we stuck closely to our text, the sixteenthly, or thereabout, would be Napanoch, but we will now shake the dust of the highway from our feet and take a woods road over the hill to Honk Lake. Down in the depths sings the Vernoy Kill, while close at hand, or under foot, were wild azalea, strawberry blossoms and other delectable matters, and on every hand was fresh young birch for the nibbling. At one point was spread a typical picture of the region up the valley of the Kill, a distant background of hills just visible through the mist, the nearer slopes wild and rugged rock and bush, with a group of dark pines in the hollow to accentuate the misty distance.

Now, just as the map said, there came a fork in the road, the middle tine of which was for me, and shortly came the Rondout, on whose bank by the roadside stood an inviting well of pure water. There is nothing that so satisfies as such a draught under such circumstances.

Turning to the left here the creek is crossed at the head of Honk Lake, on whose dark surface floated the skiffs of many patient fishermen. Just after crossing the stream we come upon the site of the "fort at Lackawack", as recently established by Mr Brink and Mr. Benedict.

Col. John Cantine, whose command lay at Lackawaxen, as a frontier guard, shifted his troops nearer to the seat of trouble in August, 1778, building a log fort about where the road now runs along the western side of Honk Lake, this following the old Indian trail, but the name of his old post was retained as Lackawack, apparently as a matter of identification. Col. Cantine sometimes dated his report from "Hunk", sometimes from Lackawack. There appears to be no record of any attack on the fort or fighting in its immediate vicinity, but it was the centre of the horse patrol, which picketed the border from Peenpack to Shandaken at the time when Burgoyne and Lord Howe were attempting the capture of the Hudson Valley.

The road now makes a point of getting down to the foot of Honk Falls as rapidly as possible and, once there, the traveler can readily understand why. The falls, some 60-70 feet high, come dashing down the sloping rocks, an avalanche of foam. Man has interfered very little with the wild beauty of the place. The trees still cling to the steep sides of this cleft in the rocks, the bottom of which is a tumble of great blocks of stone which keep the water agitated. A footpath worn along the eastern bank of the stream brings one to a fair view of the top of the falls, but the most attractive view is part way up its western border where a rock shelf juts out commanding a full view of the wild beauty. The place must be much as it was in the days of the red man, a romantic spot fit for legend and story. Being translated, Honk Falls is Falls Falls, for hunk, as it was formerly spelled, was Indian for falling water. Is that where the slang expression "to get hunk" with the enemy comes from? One is always ready to take a fall out of him if possible.

We are in Napanoch where the Sandburg and Rondout Creeks become one. The name probably means "land overflowed by water". The highway in the eastern edge of the village is known as "Lost Corners"—there is no apparent corner and nothing lost, so far as can be seen, but the name is supposed to come from a sharp turn in the creek here and the fact that land has been cut out by freshets. Here is an old building, now used as an icehouse, which dates back full two hundred years. It is locally known as the "old fort". Mr. Benedict believes that it was probably stockaded and used as a place of refuge. It was erected by the brothers Bevier, the first white settlers at this spot.

Louis Ravine, or hole, mentioned in "The Indians, or Narratives of Massacres", etc., as the place to which the inhabitants of Naponoch fled when no Indian pursued, is the ravine immediately back of the reformatory.

At each fort in the valley one man was always on guard so long as there was any possibility of Indian raid, and it was his duty, when anything suspicious was seen, to fire his gun (it was against the law to fire a gun otherwise than as a signal of danger or in self defense). The signal would be taken up by each guard in turn, and thus in a few moments the alarm was spread from one end of the valley to another, thus giving the inhabitants an opportunity to seek safety in the nearest fort.

The old "Holland guns" used by the early settlers sent forth a boom that was easily distinguishable above the crack of the smaller and lighter arm used by the Indians, and so long as the boom of these great guns could be heard during a fight, it was known that the white men were holding their own. Mr. Ronk possesses one of these weapons, which is fully six feet long and has a bore like a 10-gauge shotgun; in fact this particular gun is the one used by Cornelius Bevier during the attack on Wawarsink, and it was with this that he just did not kill two Indians with one shot, as noted in "The Indians", etc.

Mr. Isaiah Rose, of Naponoch, tells me that the old tomahawk-scarred pulpit of the stone church at Wawarsing, that is commonly supposed to have been burned with the church, was removed from the old church some time before its destruction and brought to Napanoch and stored in the cellar of the church here. The then janitor of the Napanoch church, a mere boy, has confidentially confided the fact to Mr. Rose that one cold morning when he needed kindling to start his fire the old pulpit disappeared. The lad had no appreciation of the historic value of the battered old piece of furniture.

A spring on the river bank immediately back of the hotel in Napanoch gave the Indian name of Topatcoke to the low land here. "To" is Indian for pot, and was applied here because of the peculiarity of the spring, in that while it seemed to boil up, it never overflowed its banks.

A similar spring about a mile up the mountain above Louis Ravine gave the same Indian name to that locality. The meaning of the full name is hidden from me.

Just across the Rondout on the way to Ellenville stands the simple frame cottage which is pointed out as the birthplace of De Witt Clinton.

Somewhere between here and Ellenville village once on a time lived an old woman commonly known as Floor—possibly an abbreviation for Flora, possibly a nick-name, because she could floor most of her men neighbors. Mr. Isaiah Rose remembers to have heard his mother tell how "Floor" could pick up a barrel of cider and drink from the bung. His own mother could pick up a barrel of flour and carry it, which is more than her son can do, so he says.

Well, back among the trees of the Ellenville burial ground stands a simple stone which perpetuates the fact that "Aunt Dina Hasbrouck Died Oct. 10, 1875, aged over 100 y'rs. She remembered the burning of Kingston by British troops, Oct. 1777".

I spent a day in Ellenville, mostly running over files of the Journal, and thus came by the following valuable piece of information, which a recent Journal had gleaned from one of fifty-five years ago:—

"A young fellow, a Nova Scotian, got on one of the river steamboats who was only nineteen years of age, stood seven feet and nine inches high and weighed four hundred pounds. He had not attained his full growth"—there was more of it, but that is all we need. Now, as I take it, the lesson to be learned by this is that fifty-five years ago a river steamboat that was only nineteen years of age stood seven feet nine inches high and weighed four hundred pounds was something of a novelty, but I am much puzzled over the fact that this wonderful vessel had not attained full growth; here it seems is meat for an antiquarian investigation for some gentleman of leisure. Travelers who have been to the Yosemite and to Switzerland tell how the view from the top of Shawangunk surpasses anything to be seen in those regions—why they do it is not divulged, but that they do it is not questioned. This is the country of the falling water. Every little stream, and there are many of them, no matter how high up on the mountain it rises, is sure to make for the valley just as rapidly as the atmosphere will let it, and consequently each is a series of falls and cascades.

"Cloud upon cloud, the purple pinewoods cling to the the rich
Arcadian mountains,
All the hues of the gates of heaven flashed from the white enchanted fountains
Where in the flowery glades of the forest the rivers that sing
to Arcadia spring."
—[Alfred Noyes.

As one enters the village from the north, the monument commemorating the Fantine Kill massacre is seen on the left. The Indians had learned of the proposed expedition of Generals John Sullivan and James Clinton into their own country and, led by Brant, proposed to give the whites plenty to do nearer home. The attacks on Fantine Kill, May 4th, 1779, and at Minisink on July 22d of the same year, were part of this plan. The Kill flows through the northern skirts of the village and it was along its banks that the first settlers here seem to have lodged; these were the families of Jesse Bevier, the widow of Isaac Bevier and Michael Sax. The two latter families were killed every one, except a feeble minded daughter of Mrs. Bevier, but the house of Jesse Bevier was successfully defended. The attack occurred about daybreak.

During the latter part of 1906 there appeared in the New York papers notices of the discovery of the "Old Spanish Mine" in the Shawangunk Mountain. According to these "Tradition said that from the tunnel ran a stream of living water, and Professor Mather, State Geologist of Ohio, who investigated, accepted the theory that the work was done by Spaniards who formed a part of the Ponce de Leon expedition. After failing to find the Fountain of Youth in Florida, and following their leader's dying injunction to continue the search, they are thought to have made the journey northward.

"When they came to a stream larger than a man's arm rushing out of solid rock, with no visible source of supply, they halted and began to tunnel to locate the pool whence it came. This was in the sixteenth century. The tunnel was known till recently only by Indian legend.

"One Hinsdale, finding a stream that never varied in its flow or temperature, employed a force of men and uncovered an accumulation of debris. Then he located the mouth of the tunnel itself. It is perfectly formed and the stream gushes from a fissure at the extreme end.

"The tunnel is five hundred feet long, six feet high, four feet wide and straight as an arrow, with only a rise of seven feet in its entire length."

That is the way the newspapers reported it to us. There was a mine, possibly worked in a crude way by Indians, in pre-Dutch days; this was close to the canal lock in Ellenville. When the canal was a-digging, about 1824, it was either discovered by some of the Digger White-men or its whereabouts made known to them by a local tribe, and they, after the manner of men, concluded to seek for the precious metal, whatever it might be. So a few dollars was contributed and men set to work pecking at hard-hearted old Shawangunk, but a pickaxe on the old fellow's rock ribs makes little impression, and a brief period of such work was enough to cool the ardor of the most enthusiastic. Then came those of larger views, who proposed to purchase several hundred kegs of powder, store them at the far end of the tunnel, which was some three to four hundred feet in extent, tamp it thoroughly and then touch the match which would make the rocks and the mountain to all flee away. The explosion would not only loosen the bowels of Ulster County, but was to give New England a shake, while all the world wondered.

But about now the canal folks stepped in with an injunction which even the best black powder must respect, and soon the project was forgotten, and later the mine itself, the entrance caved in, bushes and trees grew up, completely hiding all traces of the ancient diggings.

Folks have a way of dying in Ellenville and a new generation arose who knew not the Spanish Mine. So completely was its memory obliterated that when, some thirty years later, traces of lead and silver were discovered in nearby rocks and a new mine was opened, it was done in ignorance of the earlier effort; this time also much more money was sunk in the ground than was brought therefrom and another set of men were poorer and wiser, while the old mine slept on.

Then came a professor who knew a thing or two. He was to investigate the later mine as an adjunct to the Columbia School of Mines, and while poking around in the inquisitive way professors have, he stumbled on a spring of water that, to his scientific mind, was in some manner different from what a spring in such a place ordinarily is, and the professor put a padlock on his talking machine and started a little investigation on the professor's account, after which, like the man in the parable, he sold all that he had and bought that field, and then the professor took off the padlock, and now a hundred-thousand-dollar plant is going up, for the water is more excellent even than that famed soap, which is but 99-44-100 pure.

So much for the facts. What follows is not so well authenticated and may not interest those who prefer dry statistics as above, to what reads more like fiction.

Legend of the Old Spanish Mine.—Long before the Dutch knew the "Great River of the Mountains" as Henry Hudson so poetically and accurately named it, a Spanish galleon bound for the gold of Peru met contrary breezes which wafted the ship far from its course. Great damage was done to ship and rigging, and when an unknown coast came in view a harbor was diligently sought, but the long sandy stretch of shore offered no safe anchorage and the Spaniard coasted north against an icy wind that froze his thin blood and finally found an opening where the good ship lay at rest behind what we now know as Sandy Hook, but this was no place for repairs and an exploration was started up the great bay, and by little and little the bay narrowed to a great river, whose rocky shores forbade the thought of pulling the little vessel out for repairs, and so with the spirit of adventure newly awakened, the black beards kept on and on until finally they came to a sandy, shelving shore with the great forest at hand for the making of new spars for the patched sails and planks for the damaged hull.

A copper colored people, who wore furs and feather robes, gathered to see this wonder. Every man came armed with primitive weapons, but so friendly were they that the visitors were soon on the best of terms with the Indians, who brought game and corn and in return received trinkets that appealed to their sense of the esthetic. Among these trinkets were some bright copper baubles that when the natives saw immediately excited a great powwow, much gesticulation and many pointings toward the distant mountains. The Spaniards, on gold intent, drew such conclusions from these antics as pleased them most, and by signs finally made their new found friends understand that they wished to be taken over the mountain where the glitter grew.

And so repairs finished and the ship launched, an expedition was started toward the golden unknown. The sailors found that threading the rock fastnesses of the Shawangunk was quite a different matter from pacing level Spanish decks, and more than one fell by the way, for life was unimportant when gold was leading the dance.

It was a toilsome journey for those used only to the level decks of a vessel, but once over the hills our adventurers found themselves amidst great fields of growing corn in a beautiful rich valley that warmed every heart, and now the expedition turned south, following a well worn footpath along the bank of a beautiful rushing stream until the guides, turning aside among the trees, stopped, and lo! before the excited explorers was a shaft into the hillside.

Getting out the ore was a simple job, but how to get it to the smelter was a complicated question. To transport it the way they had come was manifestly impossible; a road must be found and the dusky friends were again appealed to, and now they led down the valley to our Rondout and passed its fertile meadows to the great river, and so the first white feet pressed the Old Mine Road, an older Indian trail.

The forests contributed more water then than do the ravaged lands of to-day, and it was thought that light flat boats could be floated from mine to ship, but this proved impracticable and a road was constructed. Then rumors of more mine holes were brought to the greedy adventurers, and while some delved others explored, finally locating another mine in the country of the Minisinks, and the road was extended to meet the new want.

The recently discovered documents which, while sadly mutilated, tell us this, end suddenly, almost in the middle of a sentence, but before they quite cease there are indications that the natives had grown cold and that trouble was brewing, and the supposition is that the red men finally fell on the gold seekers and slew them every one.

But all this occurred so long ago that there was no tradition concerning these happenings among the Indians on the second coming of the whites, and we must rest content with the story as it is.

The following events occurred so far back that there are probably few who now recall them; hence a brief statement of the known facts is given to introduce what has never been more than whispered before:—

A young telegraph operator, one David M. Smith, who was in the office of the canal company, disappeared suddenly on a Saturday night in February, 1866, and so completely that no trace of him could be found.

Through an odd combination of circumstances, those in Ellenville supposed he had gone for a short visit to his mother who lived near the covered bridge at Port Jackson, while the mother, though expecting him, presumed he had been detained by extra work. Thus for an entire week his disappearance was not discovered, and when the search was taken up the trail was cold.

There was no reason why he should have voluntarily dropped out in such a mysterious manner. And then he took nothing with him—even left certain letters that should have been destroyed or carried off.

Smith was well liked by young and old, but was something of a roysterer and had some evil companions but no enemies, except possibly one Flicker, a German, with whom he had quarreled over a girl, and who later went crazy and eventually died in the asylum at Ovid.

Prolonged search and even advertising failed to discover

the slightest clew to his whereabouts, and the case was finally passed into the list of unexplained mysteries.

Thirteen years later, in March, 1879, the old Ulster lead mine was reopened, after having lain idle many years, and when the debris was removed from the entrance, human remains were found which were identified as those of Smith.

Up to the time of removing this debris the only access to the drift of the old mine was by means of a shaft which led straight down from among the rocks of the mountain side to its inner end, the outer end having been effectually choked by fallen rocks.

It was recalled that the night of the disappearance was bitter cold; the point at which the shaft opened among the rocks was rough and inaccessible, and it was wholly unlikely that Smith would have gone to such a spot on such a night.

This is all that is known.

What follows appears to have been kept quiet, and few ever had any knowledge of this strangest part of the tale, though it must have at least in part reached the editor of the Journal, as in the issue of March 28, 1879, he says: "No measures have been taken to ascertain the manner of young Smith's death, * * * and nothing is likely to be done about it, although * * * a solution of the mystery would not require a miracle by any means."

The company soon supplied the vacancy made by Smith's disappearance with a young woman from a New York school, this being her first post; but she proved quick and capable and soon had the details of her work well in hand.

Now there had been a one-sided love affair, in which this girl had taken a disinterested part, the enthusiasm mostly lying with a youth attending the school with her. However, it takes a good deal to dampen the fires of young love, and as the lad was the first of the two to graduate into a position, he slipped a picture of himself between the leaves of a book belonging to the girl, in the hope that some time it might help to turn the tide in his favor.

As it happened the young man secured a position with the canal company in Port Jervis and, of course, was in daily touch with Ellenville. He knew of the disappearance of Smith and of the employment of a young woman in his stead, but did not get her name and never suspected that this was his first and only love.

So much by way of introduction.

As it will serve no good purpose to give the girl's name, she will be known in this narrative as Miss Smith. She made friends with every one who came in contact with her, including the German, Flicker, who was one of her earliest admirers, and who frightened off a number of the more timid youth who apparently thought they had an inkling that she was made for them.

Flicker was a newly made man from the moment of his acquaintance with Miss Smith. A younger son of a good family and well educated, he had long ago gone to the dogs, losing every outward sign of refinement, and his old acquaintances hardly knew him in this, to them, new role, while the girl's first impression of dislike rapidly changed to one of a wholly different nature, even before she was fully aware of it and when, in one of her idle moments, he dropped in and began a conversation which opened wide her eyes with astonishment and pleasure at his evident refinement, the battle was half won.

But while they were yet talking a most singular and uncanny thing happened: The telegraph key began to click, but in a fashion that even to a novice indicated something unusual, and the girl was puzzled and somewhat frightened, exclaiming: "This is extraordinary—terrible! No human being can be at the other end of this wire; but, whoever it is, he says murder has been committed. Much I cannot make out; only now and then a word or a phrase. [Then reading]: 'I was thrown down a deep h-o-l-e i-n t-h-e r-o-c-k-s a-n-d m-y'—— now it is unintelligible again." Flicker was at first frightened beyond the power of moving, but managed to cover his confusion and left as quickly as possible.

It was some days before he ventured around again, but when he did he was met by a curious look and a remark that some very singular and disjointed messages had been coming to her that constantly warned her against some German, whose name she never caught. The operator at times telegraphed like a professional but complained that he was lying doubled up and had not the free use of his hand. The horror again crept over Flicker, but he pulled himself together and asked if she had the name of the operator. No; she had asked for it, but could not untangle the answer.

Oddly enough she could not tell whether the messages came from the north or the south, but was strongly of the impression that they came down an almost disused line that ran up the mountain side, until she learned that there was no one along this line now. The instrument clicked again and she read: "H-e- i-s n-o-w w-i-t-h"——. "There", said she, "how is it possible to make anything out of that?" But Flicker had vanished.

The German kept away for a long time and the strange messages ceased. But now another inexplicable thing happened. The young man at Port Jervis awoke one night from a sound sleep with a feeling that he was wanted, but where or by whom he had no intimation. He was, however, impelled to dress and go out into the stillness of the night. Naturally he walked toward the telegraph office—his steps led that way every day—and as naturally he unlocked the door and entered, and was surprised to hear the click of his instrument. There was then no night work along the line and no one ever thought of calling up after hours.

The key clicked out: "Y-o-u a-r-e w-a-n-t-e-d, t-h-e-r-e i-s n-o t-i-m-e t-o b-e l-o-s-t, t-h-e o-n-e y-o-u l-o-v-e i-s i-n d-a-n-g-e-r." He called back to know who it was and where, but the only answer was: "H-e-r-e. H-u-r-r-y! h-u-r-r-y!! h-u-r-r-y!!!" There was an indescribable manner in the sending of the message that thrilled the young fellow. He never doubted but that it was intended for him and that the one he was to help was his only love, for he had not forgotten her; but what could he do? Where was she? Could she be an operator up the line? There was the girl at Ellenville—he had never known who she was. It flashed on him like an inspiration, and without stopping to reason the matter out he started for his saddle horse, an old friend and tough, who was accustomed to some pretty rough traveling.

To saddle the horse and start for the towpath of the canal —the best bridle path in the world, and one he was well acquainted with for a large part of the thirty odd miles to be covered—was but the work of a few moments. His excitement was quickly communicated to the horse and they were soon racing through the night, the rider doing all he could to ease the work of the animal, knowing that the strain would be very great before the end came.

It began to be noticed that Flicker was growing more and more moody. He had long ago forsaken his old haunts, but now he was never seen except as his work required it, and he was known to spend his Sundays and spare time by himself in the woods, but most people rather feared, and none liked, him. Thus he went his own way undisturbed and was little seen and less missed.

Presumably in one of these rambles he discovered a sort of cave formed by fallen rock masses in a secluded ravine, in the back part of which was a peculiar spring that apparently boiled up, yet never ran over, similar to those that have given Indian names to the flats at Napanoch and to a part of the mountain above. Just when the idea came to Flicker is, of course, not known, but he evidently conceived the crazy notion of abducting the girl to this cave and holding her prisoner until she would consent to marry him, as later discoveries showed he stocked the place with necessaries enough to last months.

And now everything in readiness, he began to lay his plans. He regularly watched the girl go back and forth between her home and office until he knew every inch of the route; he also paid attention to the house, which stood near the canal, a short half mile south of the telegraph office, until he knew the room she occupied and just what other rooms were used as bedrooms—knew the habits of all its people, in fact no little detail lacked attention. And on the very night that the strange message came to Port Jervis, Flicker had prepared to carry out his plan.

One of the inmates of the house was taken sick this night and it was not until 2 o'clock that the last light went out and all was still, and by 2 o'clock horse and rider were passing through Wurtsboro, only twelve miles away. The pace had been a fast one and both were well done up. Many people had risen from their beds to gaze out into the darkness and wonder who it was and what the trouble.

Flicker thought that a half hour should be sufficient for all to be asleep, and in due time proceeded to the window of the girl's room, but found that a screen placed therein had been fastened, and it took twenty minutes or more to remove this. Then he had disturbed the sleeper and must wait for her to quiet again. Horse and rider by now are sweeping down through Spring Glen. Finally the abductor entered the room, smothered the girl's cries, and before she could make a sound was out of the window with his prize in his arms.

The night had been dark and starless; there had been some lightning on the horizon; but even while the desperado was at work the storm so rapidly approached that the incessant thunder drowned every other sound and the telegraph wires becoming surcharged with the electric fluid blazed with a steady light, enough to readily illumine the path and the canal. The storm had terrified the already wild horse, until every ounce of strength was put into this, his last mad run, and as the pair bore down on him, the startled German only saw an avenging angel flashing down from on high, to his startled vision a huge god scourging his horse with the forked lightning which seemed to emanate from the raised hand, and believing his time had come he relinquished his hold on the girl and fled.

To transfer the girl back to the shelter of the house was but the work of a moment, but to the anxious lover it seemed long hours before she was returned to consciousness again. Then the young couple had an all too short moment together, but though brief there was time for hurried explanations and a prompt yes, and soon the minister replaces the doctor.

The wild night has gone out in peace, the air is full of sunshine and the damp smell of the woods; but matters must still move rapidly for the young couple. There is no leave of absence at Port Jervis. Fortunately, however, a substitute is at hand for Ellenville, and such a bridal party as the old canal never bore before was floating swiftly southward while a very tired horse, gaily decked with the bridal wreath, was placidly munching sugar with his oats and paying small attention to the swiftly changing beauties of nature which were spread around with such lavish hand. And so ends a very singular little romance.

The Leuren Kill as seen by the author.

LEUREN KILL TO BASHA'S KILL.

The twenty-eighth milestone stands within the southern confines of Ellenville.

Some two miles out of Ellenville the Leuren Kill crosses the road. The name, it is said, means "Trading Post Brook", hence it is to be supposed that in the early days there was a country store here, but apparently there is not even a tradition concerning it. Back from the road and near the bank of the Kill, but not to be seen from the highway, stands a house that looks as though it was one of the old guard. This was built at the beginning of the French and Indian War by Conrad Bevier, so says the widow of his grandson, Cornelius, who died thirty years ago. Mrs. Bevier, who now lives in Ellenville, tells the following story: One night during the French and Indian War, Conrad Bevier was called to Wawarsing and was compelled to leave his wife alone in the house. A good supply of wood was provided, the windows were securely fastened by blocks of wood and the door heavily barred.

During the dark hours a party of about six Indians attempted to enter the house, and on failing to break through, climbed to the roof with intent to descend by the chimney, but Mrs. Bevier anticipating thus had kept a hot fire burning, which amply protected this means of ingress. The Indians, however, being endowed with the virtues of patience and hope, waited in the belief that the supply of wood could not hold out, remaining constantly on the roof, and sure enough the wood did run low and the fire began to die down. But Mrs. Bevier had prepared for this emergency by ripping open two mattresses stuffed with straw, and when the Indians made the attempt to enter she sent a roaring flame up the chimney which gave them pause. Several times they made the attempt, but each time were met in the same way, and finally as morning began to dawn the assailants drew off.

Conrad Bevier later sold this house and built the stone house which to-day stands well back from and south of the main road in Napanoch (not the "Old Fort").

The old house on the Leurenkill may have been sold to a Newkirk, certainly a member of this family occupied it at an early date, then came the Freers under its roof, then the Brodheads, and for the last fifty years it has been in the possession of the Jackson S. Schultz family, of New York.

Rev. Matt. C. Julien remembers hearing his mother (born 1809) tell of the parties for which the house was celebrated throughout the countryside when she was a girl; in her time it was known as the Brodhead house. There is a delicate little fall in the Kill near the house, and a rough bridge, all of which looked good to the camera, but the result indicated that color had more to do with the picture than had light and shade.

Possibly a mile beyond the Leurenkill stands the old Brodhead house—1753. The rising generation (he has yet some distance to rise, as he has only been at it ten or a dozen years) is the ninth in the Brodhead line that has inhabited the house without a break.

The house was, of course, loopholed, but sixty or more years ago it was rejuvenated as to its outer walls with a coat of "dash", and of course the loopholes were then plastered over.

Probably it was at this time that the old double Dutch door, which bore silent witness of Indian attack in numerous hacks made by their tomahawks, disappeared into the kindling wood pile.

Across the road on a slight elevation are the graves of forty-six of the Brodhead slaves. And the women folks say that so recently as within a month or two, more or less, they have seen a bear in the corn patch opposite—it was surely a bear because it was black and acted like one—though those made of sterner stuff incline to sniff at the suggestion, hinting that it was merely a black dog gone astray. However, I prefer to think that it was a bear.

In October, 1757, a few Cayugas persuaded some of the Indians along the Delaware to join them in a raid. On the 12th they appeared at the house of Peter Jan, in what is now Sullivan County. Two soldiers posted in the neighborhood as scouts were killed, as also one of Jan's daughters. Jan and two sons, at work in a field, escaped. Another soldier in the house with Jan's wife and two remaining daughters, successfully defended the place, and when the Indians retired he took the woman and girls to the house of Captain Brodhead, a mile distant. The Indians then returned and burned the Jan house.

This was a glorious day after the storm. Old Shawangunk looked like an Indian chief wrapped in his cloak of feathers. The foliage was just beginning to open—it is the month of May—so that, including the blue above, there are all the colors of the rainbow, possibly subdued a bit. More varieties of greens and yellows and reds than could be counted: it is all scrub except for an occasional tall dark spruce that looked like a buttonhole in the old fellow's jacket. Beneath him was spread a fine green velvet carpet, woven in pictures of meadow lands with houses and cattle, stone walls and files of trees, a great picture of prosperity and plenty.

At first our way leads up the valley of the Sandberg Creek, and when that takes to the woods at Spring Glen the Homowack takes its place. This is Indian for "the water runs out", and may refer to the fact that this is the crown of the valley from which the water flows both north and south, for it is not long before we take up with Basha Kill which, with the help of the Neversink, eventually finds its way into the Delaware, as the Homowack does into the Hudson.

At Phillipsport the old canal bed comes over to our side of the valley, and we are treated to a series of abandoned locks and canal scenes. At one point a brook of considerable volume has made itself at home in the old canal bed.

A brief outline of the romance of the Delaware and Hudson Canal is interesting, for even in such a dry document as a State Engineer's Report (see Appendix) a thread of romance insists on weaving its way through the statistics.

A Philadelphia merchant who enjoyed close communion with nature makes his way on foot up into the northeastern corner of his state with knapsack and blanket and an axe in his belt for the evening's firewood, camping where night overtakes him, apparently not for the purpose of hunting or even fishing, but because of his love of the freedom and the grandeur of mountain and forest.

And as he walks he notes a black stone cropping out here and there and, being of an inquiring turn of mind, though no geologist, he picks up a piece now and then, taking a few bits home where he and his brothers learn somehow that it will burn; then being thrifty and persistent the Wurts brothers desire to know more about this curiosity, and William goes back and manages to get out a few tons, builds him a raft and attempts to get his "stone-coal" down the river for the further enlightenment of his brothers and himself.

After losing several cargoes against rocks, or amidst rapids, by persistent effort he manages finally to get a raft through. His neighbors seem to have looked on his foolish waste of effort with smiling toleration, but with an unconcern that must have been exasperating to the enthusiast, though it dampened not his ardor. We can imagine him going about among his friends telling how this black stone burned and gave out a good heat and must have great value; but most folks had burned wood, and their fathers before them; wherefore then should they fly in the face of Providence by going against the traditions of their fathers? Fie on the dreamer! We will none of him.

But the Wurts brothers had long heads as well as enthusiasm. Land was cheap in that far country; they would take a flier of a few thousand acres; something might come of it—and they did. Further experiments only convinced them the more, and they mined and shipped down stream to their own city and the south, for by now other people were discovering coal and the public was beginning to find out that it was good to burn, and the market, though small, was worth cultivating.

The first known experiment in burning coal in this country was that of a blacksmith, in 1769, but so little did he think of the result that it was not until forty years later that he tried the burning of it in a grate for fuel. During the Revolution it was used by the blacksmiths in the armory at Carlisle, Pa. In 1792 the Lehigh Coal Mining Company was formed, but it did little more than purchase lands. Then come the Wurts brothers' experiments about 1812, and about this same time

Col. George Shoemaker took nine wagonloads to Philadelphia, but could not sell it. It was soon after used with success in rolling mills in Delaware County, and from then on began to be used elsewhere. But it was not until 1825 that the trade took on proportions that would warrant the non-enthusiast to venture in with his capital.

But the Wurts brothers were still years ahead of their neighbors, for they saw a market for their product in New York and began a hunt for the means of reaching that market, and so the Delaware and Hudson Canal was conceived in the brain of the dreamer. People laughed at the suggestion. Here were a thousand feet to be climbed and a thousand unknown difficulties to be overcome through a rugged wilderness, but Maurice Wurts, who seems to have been the leader in the family, evidently had the persuasive tongue of conviction; he believed and he made others believe. A company was formed and surveys prosecuted, estimates secured, the scheme was presented to the Legislatures of Pennsylvania and New York and the Legislators won over, and even yet the extended use of coal was problematical, for it was still some years to 1825.

The canal is built after a fashion and water let in, but too much gravel has been used in the banks and the water seeps out and the I-told-you-sos clap their little hands with joy. It is two years more before water is again allowed to find its way into the canal, and the canal is a success. Then comes the cholera scare in New York, that hurts; the panic of 1833-4, that hurts. The first coal shipped was surface coal of inferior quality, that hurts; jealous rivals who begin to fear the unceasing push, push, push of the enthusiastic genius who, through all these long years of doubt has never taken his shoulder from the wheel, combine to work against the success of the scheme, but they are working against the relentless fate that always keeps its powder dry. Wall Street attacks the stock, but still the work goes on.

In 1832 a small dividend comes as a welcome Christmas present to the long expectant stockholders, but not until 1839 is there another such bright spot on the horizon. After this the dividends are steady, 8 per cent for years, except in 1842 when they arose to 10 per cent. When the $800,000 of state loans come due, a large sum for those days, the canal pays off every cent without a wink. It is free of incumbrance and by now earning from 10 to 24 per cent per annum; the capital stock has grown from $500,000 to $10,000,000. Is there no romance in the dry bones of statistics?

At the foot of Council Hill I fell in with two small boys, who were on their way to the village to look for father. It seems that father likes to talk and is apt to forget how the time flies when he meets a friend, and this was the day when the family was to return home to Middletown, and it was already afternoon. We jogged along comfortably together, none of us in any great hurry. The boys knew where there were some ripe grapes a piece down the road and we stopped here long enough to gather two small caps full (a minute ago it was the month of May, but just now we are in September). Then there was an apple tree which offered some attractive looking red-cheeked fruit, and that occupied a few minutes. Otherwise we kept going at a fair pace, barring an occasional well or a farmer, from whom I hoped to gather information.

Some two miles before Wurtsboro stood until two years ago the old Devens blockhouse, or fort, built in 1757 by Conrad Bevier. And near this same spot, behind a barn on the right, as one goes south, stands the blueflag tombstone of

"Manuel Gonsalus is Gestorven De 18 April Anno 1758", which means that the gentleman died so long ago. He is known as the first white settler, though he was probably sixty to seventy years behind the first settler. His son Sam was a noted character during the Revolution.

The Gonsalus family kept a log tavern here and they also built a sawmill. Both tavern and mill were undoubtedly the first within the limits of Sullivan County.

It is also in this immediate neighborhood that the Shawanoesberg or Council Hill is located. Here was the lodge in which the neighboring clans held their councils and here, according to a tradition of the Mamakating Indians, a bloody battle occurred between the local tribes and the Senecas in which the former were victorious, though others have it that they were badly licked.

Of the road from Esopus to Minisink we find the following:

"General Assembly, Die Sabbati, May 11th, 1734.

"The petition of Jacobus Swartwout, Wm. Provost, Wm. Cool and others, freeholders and inhabitants residing and living in Minisink, in the county of Orange and Ulster, was presented to the House, etc., setting forth that several persons in West Jersey and Penna., having no other way to transport their produce than through the Minisink road and there was but about 40 miles more to repair, before they come to Esopus, etc.; that they be compelled to work on said road and assist in repairing it to the house of Egbert Dewitt, in the town of Rochester, in the county of Ulster.

"Resolved, That leave be given to bring in a bill according to the prayer of the petition."

This road ran through the valley of the Mamakating, which

name applied about as far north as the Council Hill above mentioned.

Mr. Ruttenber writes that what was originally known as the "Mamacottin path" is more modernly known as the Old Mine Road, which was opened as a highway in 1756.

During the Revolution a line of block-houses was built through this valley under the superintendence of James Clinton, brother of the first Governor of the State. These were garrisoned by soldiers who patrolled the valley and acted as scouts.

The following letter, now owned by Benj. C. Swartwout, of Huguenot, and which I understand has never been published, is interesting in this connection:—

"Sir "Fort Montgomery 20th May 1777.

"I have received your letter of the 29th together with one of the 15th Instant from Tyler & Lassly at Casheghton. I shall at all Times be willing to afford Aid & Protection to every Part of the State which the Nature of my Command & the Trust reposed in me will permit. In the Present Case I Cant think the Information given by our Friends at Casheghton will warrant calling out the Militia, especially in this Busy Season of the Year. It amounts to no more than that two or three Traitors have been in that Neighborhood & were guilty of Insolent Expressions in that the well disposed Inhabitants were Jealous they were tampering with the Indians or on some other Bad Intent.

"I would advise our Friends to take those Persons up & send them here and if any evidence of their Guilt can be offered they will not readily trouble them a second Time. Indeed it is my Opinion that it is too late to wait for advice what steps to pursue with our Internal Enemies; if we don't destroy or Confine them they will us.

"I am your
most
Obed't Servt.

"George Clinton.

"To Philip Swartwout, Esqr.
"Chairman of the Committee of Pienpack."

Over on the other side of the valley from the highway flows Basha's Kill, concerning whose delectabilities I find the following remark: "Perhaps the trout of no stream in the world are superior to those of Basha's Kill. One hundred years ago a man could catch as many there in an hour or two as he could carry. At certain seasons of the year salmon came to the same stream from the ocean."

Tradition says Basha was an Indian squaw, queen of her tribe or clan, who lived on the banks of the stream, and some investigator has suggested that the name may be the Dutch diminutive for Elizabeth, but I have found identically the same name on Martha's Vineyard, Mass., as the name of an Indian squaw, and certainly there was no Dutch influence on that island, even if Adrian Block did clap his eyes on it in the long ago. The stream has also been known as Pine Kill.

As I saw Basha's Kill at Wurtsboro in the half light of early evening some boys were driving the cows home and as they paused for a moment in the cooling flood, the picture brought to mind so vividly the work of George Inness that it seemed quite natural to look down in the grass of the foreground for his signature.

WURTSBORO AND ROUND THERE.

We are about due at Wurtsboro, named after one of the chief promoters of the D. & H. Canal, Maurice Wurts. When the Yankees swarmed over the hills into this valley they counted the mountain peaks in sight and called the place Rome, which name it retained as late as 1812, in which year the first church building was erected, Dutch Reformed, and this building was christened the "Church of Rome", a somewhat prophetic christening, for the Catholics gobbled it in the course of time. Now the manner of the christening was peculiar to the day and generation, and all right then, though it appears in these thrifty times somewhat wasteful. It seems that when the framework was raised and the building had assumed definite shape, a workman climbed to the highest point with a jug of the best rum the country afforded, and when at the peak he swung the jug a certain number of times around his head and then threw it to the ground, the name of the church being proclaimed aloud as the good liquor was spilled over mother earth.

The postoffice here was Mamakating, the place being popularly known as "Mammy Cotton Holler" until about 1825, when the change was made to Wurtsboro as noted above.

While stopping for a moment to admire a Wurtsboro lane with apple blossom accompaniment and debating with the camera as to the picture possibilities here spread out, along

The Bevier house on the Leuren Kill (*above*). The Brodhead house, which dates from 1753, about a mile beyond Leuren Kill (*below*). Both photos from Hine's collection.

The Yaugh house or hunting house spring, Wurtsboro, known to both Indians and white men and frequently noted in old surveys (*above*). Saddler's Hell, outside of Wurtsboro (*below*). Photos from Hine's collection.

came a small girl who could give the one touch needed. She agreed to pose with alacrity, thanking me kindly for the privilege, and finally went on her way without even asking to see the picture.

I lodged here with Mr. Gumaer, who appeared to have small sympathy with my idling. As his ancestors helped kill off the Indians in these parts it seemed as though there should be some tradition, or incident, or legend tucked away in his memory that I might adopt, and so started pumping, but the pump sucked from first to last, and when he finally remarked that he did not care whether his ancestors came over in a ship or a wheelbarrow, I gave him up and went down the street to seek whom I might devour with questions.

So far as can be ascertained witches have not been troublesome of late in these parts, but there was a time when they were as serious a handicap here as was formerly the case up Hurley way; but those of the Mamakating were fortunate in having a witch finder who, through some occult power not revealed to ordinary mortals, was at times able to overcome and subdue the dread devilments.

Now this is a true story of the way in which a certain witch of Wurtsboro was healed of her evil spirit. An unnamed farmer of these parts was possessed of a mare who in due course presented him with twin colts which immediately caught the fancy of the witches and they were wont to ride the new born creatures after dusk to those haunts selected for the midnight orgies—at least that is the only way to account for the condition of those colts, who were thin and weak, with manes matted and tangled. Fortunately at this point the farmer applied to the witch finder for relief and he, after carefully looking over the ground, rubbed grease in the mussed-up manes, soaped and unsnarled them, and put the young animals in pastures some distance apart.

He then returned to the house and, while at dinner, there came in one who he recognized, by virtue of that peculiar penetration of which he alone was possessed, as a witch. The witch was allowed to depart all unsuspecting that her sins had found her out, and the witch finder immediately secured a shoe from the right hind foot of the mare and placed it among the coals in the fireplace "to get het up", and the next day when the witch again dropped in she was invited to remain to dinner and, still unsuspicious of the deep laid plot that had been a hatching, accepted.

Just as she was about to sit down to the table the horseshoe, which had been heating for the past twenty-four hours, was slipped on the chair beneath her and, though she arose in a manner almost precipitate, she arose "branded a mason". Thus was she permanently cured of her fly-by-night inclination, and when it was found that the manes of the colts were in good order the witch finder was given a quart of whiskey and a silver dollar for the job, and was well paid, as I think all will agree.

The valley here has evidently filled in to a considerable extent since the ice age ceased its cutting operations. Jacob Helm, an early settler, is authority for the statement that upon removing a large white pine stump he found under this, and some five feet below the surface, another stump of a tree quite as large as the one removed. This is quite in line with the history of that older Rome, whose ruins are builded on those of earlier times.

A short half-mile before coming to the crossroads, which marks the centre of Wurtsboro, a spring flows from the bank some ten feet below the level of the road and on the east. It is easy to find if one knows just where it is, but is quite as easily overlooked otherwise, as the footpath travels the western edge of the highway. This is the Yaugh house spring, a noted watering place of the early days. There were many Yaugh or hunting houses along the frontier and the name is not very distinctive, but this particular spring was a landmark from which many a survey was started.

The Indians were from early times believed to have mined lead among the rocks of the Shawangunk, near Wurtsboro, but they refused to give up the secret of the mine. Finally a white hunter named Miller stumbled on the spot, but made no use of his discovery. The information, however, was passed on from one generation to another until about 1817, when the ore was assayed and found valuable, but title to the land could not be perfected and the location was carefully guarded by those in the secret until 1836, when one of the partners, Moses Stanton, who had an unfortunate habit of talking in his sleep, thus disposed of the secret in the hearing of his son, who then had no difficulty in finding the exact spot. "The young man found the owners (of the land) and made $500 by keeping his ears open while his father dreamed aloud."

Dr. Theodore C. Van Wyck was one of the original characters of his generation and this neighborhood. He was cultivated and courteous, but he had his own way of saying things. The Doctor, while always respectful toward religion, did not take a very lively interest in such matters; but during a revival in the Bloomingburg church it was noted that he was a frequent attendant and great hopes were entertained by the Domine that he would be added to the fold. But the Doctor seemed to hang fire somehow and it was a case of hope deferred, until finally the Domine thought the time had come to strike a blow, and while all were on their knees the good man asked the Doctor to pray. "There was a solemn pause—a grave-like silence—the tympanum of every ear was eager to catch the first utterance from the Doctor's lips. But he was as silent as a graven image. Thinking he had not heard the first request, the good man repeated it, whereupon the Doctor spoke: 'Damn it, sir! Damn it, sir! I pay you to pray, sir! you to pray, sir!'"

The Doctor had a mare who was wholly insensible to ordinary methods of acceleration, and her driver finally made a goad, the application of which was easily translated by his four-footed friend into a hurry call. The Doctor, of course, was greatly pleased, and though the feelings of the mare have not been recorded, she gave every evidence that she was sensible of his pointed attentions.

One fine day the Doctor took his small son Charles for a drive, and in honor of the event had a spirited young horse hitched to his best buggy; but he made the mistake of the day when he used that goad, for in a jiffy thereafter he and the boy were deposited by the roadside and the horse was fast disappearing in a cloud of dust. Neither were hurt, but "Charles landed where some vagrant cows had deposited plenty of the material from which modern chemists extract the 'balm of a thousand flowers'. Into and over this he rolled in such a way that he was smeared with it from head to foot." Picking the boy up, but keeping him at arm's length, the Doctor marched home and into the presence of Mrs. Van Wyck, and thus spoke: "He is not hurt, madam—not hurt; but damnably besmirched, madam—damnably besmirched."

Just how far it is from Wurtsboro to Port Jervis seems to

be open to doubt. Mr. Gumaer, above, says nineteen miles. The guide board makes it an even twenty, while the pedometer had it seventeen. Generally the pedometer agrees with my view of the situation, but this time I am inclined to look on the guide board with favor.

About the first thing I did on getting out of Wurtsboro was to cross Breakfast Brook, because the road went that way. It seems that those traveling toward Esopus were wont to rendezvous here for the morning meal, hence the name. The Dutch called it Scufftite Kiltje, which, if my guess is a good one, means the same thing. It surely does if we insert a "t" in place of the "c" immediately after the "S".

I recall seeing somewhere, during one of my Springtime jaunts through the valley, fields of sorrel in bloom, the warm reddish-brown combined with the soft, fresh green of the early season making one of the most beautiful of color schemes. I have never seen the sorrel massed as it was at this time. Sometimes an entire half acre would show nothing but the warm tones—sometimes the hand of the Artist had blended the one color into the other until it was like a shimmer of interchangeable silk, red or green, as the wind swayed the grasses.

This for a foreground, while beyond loomed old Shawangunk darkened by the fleeting shadows of the clouds, with its many warm spring tints from bursting buds. The old fellow's sides seamed into wave after wave, each strongly delineated by the slanting rays of the morning light glancing across its many ravines.

A mile out of Wurtsboro comes Page's Brook, which our highway is supposed to cross as it progresses toward the south. But to-day it is merely a spring on the right and a morass on the left of the highway; at least it is so in dry weather. A dam has been stretched across this swamp and half of it turned into a pond, but it is quite easy to see where our friend, mentioned below, found his trouble.

There was a day when this was a broad, sluggish stream, the fording of which was a nightmare to those approaching, a curse to those in its midst and a theme of vivid conversation for the remainder of the trip.

On a certain Summer's day, when the flies were aggressive and the heat uppermost, a lone saddler might have been seen approaching this slough of despond. He was mounted on a lean animal, whose ruminations no doubt ran on a snack of oats that had once crossed the path of his youth, and there was a look in his eyes that was easily translated into a great longing for green grass. But the saddler awoke the beast out of his revery with a crack over the ribs that led him to negotiate the crossing without loss of time.

Now the saddler had never been through this country before and knew not the quagmire that lay beneath the surface of the water, and when his horse came to a halt in midstream he dealt out an extra kick in the ribs and an invitation to proceed which met with but feeble response, and what little effort his animal made seemed but to accentuate his downward course, for soon the rider was compelled to draw up his feet, and soon he sat cross-legged like any tailor.

In the meantime his flow of words increased until it filled all the country side, and the saddler had no mean command of his mother tongue as he understood it. His cadences rose and fell on the atmosphere as did his stick on the shrinking ribs beneath him, but to no good purpose. Here was indeed a sad state of affairs. To stay where he was was not to be endured, for his position was hotly contested by clouds of flies and mosquitoes; to dismount was equally out of the question, for then would his feet be planted in the same sink-hole as were those of his horse. What wonder that he held converse with himself nor hesitated lest the world might hear.

So happy, copious and potent was his vocabulary that he soon attracted other travelers, who hastened forward to learn the cause of the uproar, and through their reports of the trend of his remarks came the name that long exalted this fording place above its fellows, "Roumakers Hel", or "Saddler's Hell", though I cannot find it anywhere recorded that the saddler was held responsible for the mixed condition of his language, his evident sincerity apparently atoning for any seeming lack of polish.

Shawangunk still keeps in touch with the landscape, which latter seems bent on furnishing new and varied foregrounds for the old fellow. Now it is a stone wall bordered by ferns with beautiful meadow lands beyond, then comes a brook and a patch of woods, a cluster of homes or some homely farm scene. And as one walks south the light is always changing: first the mountain is all in shadow and the cool morning air seems to come from its darkened nooks; then the sun begins to send long shafts down its rugged sides, bringing into prominence each bump and hollow. But the sun keeps climbing and the shadows shorten, and soon it is hot work pegging along in the broad glare of noonday.

WESTBROOKVILLE TO HUGUENOT.

Now the moving picture shows us Westbrookville, formerly Basha's Land, Bessie's Land or Bashasville, named for Dirck Van Keuren Westbrook, first white settler here. His is a stone house so well kept that it suggests to the passing stranger only peace and plenty and gives no hint of the dark hours of the Revolution, when it was the fort to which fled the inhabitants in time of need.

One of the patriots of the region was Elder Benjamin Montanye, of the Baptist Church. At a certain point in the game of war, when Washington felt that the next important move was to deceive the enemy as to his real intention, and he needed an absolutely trustworthy man to carry out his plans, he selected Montanye to bear fictitious dispatches to General Greene and allow himself to be captured, dispatches and all. It all fell out just as was planned and the British were so pleased with the intercepted information that they had an illumination in New York, and later a second illumination in their vacuum pans which, while possibly quite as brilliant, could hardly have held the attraction of the first. In the meantime the dispatch bearer got two months in the sugar-house prison as his reward.

Beyond Westbrookville lies ten or more miles of highway to Port Jervis, interspersed with Cuddebackville, the Neversink, Port Clinton, Huguenot (old Peenpack) and automobiles, those pests that, like an insistent fly, will not leave one alone.

Travelers along the roads hereabouts will note frequent combinations of figures painted on the stone walls; these represent the height above sea level and have been placed recently by government surveyors who have been mapping the region.

Cuddebackville (name originally spelled Caudebec) lies along our highway just before it crosses the Neversink. The canal here is kept up for a mile or more from the river for the purpose of furnishing power that is turned into electricity for the use both of Port Jervis and Middletown; this forms a beautiful stretch for boating and the old towpath makes a delightful footpath for an evening's saunterings when the long shadows lie on the floor of the valley below.

There is nothing in this immediate vicinity of story or legend, so far as has been discovered, but Benjamin Eaton once lived in a lonely cabin on the mountain side, across the valley toward Otisville, and a bronze tablet now adorns his grave in the burial ground here "To perpetuate the memory of Benjamin Eaton, who served in the Continental Army as a member of the bodyguard of General Washington, 1780-1783 'Conquer or die'."

Neversink is a corruption of the Lenape word newas, "a promontory", and ink, "at"—"at the promontory".

Where the canal crossed the Neversink stood until recently, on the south side, an old grist mill built before the Revolution by Wm. C. Rose, who came from Connecticut. This was the first of the kind in Orange County. Settlers brought their grist from as far as Wayne County, Pa., fifty miles up the Delaware Valley, packing the load on their backs through the forest. On more than one occasion the mill did service as a fort. The old discarded mill stones are yet to be seen.

Port Clinton is one of the birth places of Governor De Witt Clinton. Here is also an old Gumaer dwelling, which is locally credited with having been a fort in the days of the French and Indian War. There are two opinions, however, as to this, so are there some who likewise scoff at a small stone building which the P. C.'s would have us believe was a Revolutionary fort. It does look rather new, and has windows and lacks portholes, and altogether was a bit difficult even for me to accept, and every one knows my swallow is in the best of condition at all times.

It may seem to some that my capacity for marvels is remarkably well developed, but that is easily accounted for. My father used to remark that he could swallow anything that could get through his shirt collar, and one had but to see that shirt collar to appreciate how great was the old gentleman's ability. It began to flare the instant it left the neckband and made the finest kind of a funnel, and my progenitor did not believe in snug neckbands either. I do not wear just his kind of a collar, but mine does very well.

Here is also an old log house which does not claim to be anything but an old log house, and as such the camera accepted it.

The History of Deerpark, by Peter E. Gumaer tells us that about 1690 Jacob Cuddeback, Thomas Swartwout, Anthony Swartwout, Bernardus Swartwout, Peter Gumaer, John Tyse and David Jamison settled in Deerpark in the central part of the Peenpack flats, on a knoll about three-quarters of a mile south of the old Gumaer stone house. Fort Gumaer was located on the south end of this knoll.

The nearest settlement at that time was twenty-five to thirty miles toward Kingston. Cuddeback, Gumaer and one of the Swartwouts were the only ones who remained and they, being too weak to defend themselves against the encroaching Jerseymen, gave to Hermanus Van Inwegen a certain portion of their land, he to live thereon and help them protect their property. Van Inwegen is spoken of as bold, strong and resolute.

The historian gives an account of an almost-bewitchment about as follows: A family of Peenpack discovered one morning after a light fall of snow the tracks of a man, or what appeared to be such, on the slope of their roof where no man could walk and were greatly alarmed, fearing it a portent of disaster. Having no "Lady from Philadelphia" handy by for consultation, they did the next best thing and repaired to the house of Major James Swartwout for advice. The Major returned with the messenger and looked the roof over, and as there could be no doubt about the tracks, he turned his attention to those about him and soon singled out a slave whose actions spoke louder than words. The Major could throw a bluff as well as the next man and the slave finally confessed that he had atttached a shoe to a long pole, and with this made the tracks. It almost seems a pity that the Major should have been so wise, for he undoubtedly ruined a first-class witch story in the making.

Suppose there had been no Major to appeal to and that family had gone about its daily avocations in fear and trembling until some one had accidentally stepped on the tail of the black cat? We shudder to think what the consequences might have been.

Peenpack is probably Dutch, meaning low, soft land.

There was once an old gentleman in these parts who used to tell how a friendly Indian made known to his father and a neighbor the existence of a silver mine in the Shawangunk Mountain. These two worked the mine secretly, making frequent and mysterious journeys to dispose of the ore. When the Revolution came both went to the war, first covering the mouth of the mine with a flat stone and destroying all evidences of their work.

When war was at an end, one of the miners was dead and the other returned to find his home burned by the Indians and his family fled to a distant village. The home being re-established he set out to again work his silver mine, but the "three marked trees that stood thirty paces directly east of the entrance" had vanished in a forest fire, and his search was in vain.

Another story tells how a boy of twelve, a great friend of an Indian chief, was blindfolded and taken to the mountain and down into the mine where, when the bandage was removed, he saw a solid vein of silver. But he was returned as he came and no amount of searching could discover the treasure, but "every seven years a bright light like a candle flame, rises at 12 o'clock at night, above the mine, and disappears in the clouds". Many have seen the phenomenon and sought its source, but none have succeeded. The last time this occurred was in July, 1906, when, according to the New York papers, a "large ball of fire" hovered above old Shawangunk several nights in succession.

The French and Indian War caused great distress in this outpost region. Up to that time the whites and Indians had met without undue friction; but when, about 1755, the latter began to disappear, the settlers, knowing their treacherous character, began preparations for war by sending the women and children away. Three forts were built in the Peenpack neighborhood and three next to the Delaware. The first were located, one on the Neversink not far from Cuddebackville, one at the house of Peter Gumaer and one at the house of William Westfall.

The first hostile act was in 1756, when three men at work in the fields harvesting the crops were killed. The next was an attempt to capture the fort at Westfalls, occupied, as the Indians at the time supposed, by two lone women. But between the time of their first reconnoiter and of the attack, a party of soldiers from New Jersey had arrived at the fort, and these were just seating themselves at the table when the Indians burst in, whereupon both sets of warriors were vastly surprised; but the Indians proceeded to work and the soldiers proceeded upstairs where they shortly gathered their scattered wits and opened such a destructive fire that the invaders retired precipitately. A number were killed on each side.

The upper fort on the Neversink was surprised and burned and the entire garrison massacred.

But even before this—so far back as 1730-1740—was there border warfare through this country, but a war in which the Indians took no part. This was the war over the boundary line between New York and New Jersey, and all due to a certain vagueness of description in the charters of the provinces. The New Jersey charter carried the west bounds "along said River or Bay (Delaware) to the Northward as far as the Northwardmost branch of the said Bay or River, which is in latitude 41 deg. 40 min., and crosseth over thence in a straight line to the latitude 41 deg. on Hudson's River". The "Northwardmost branch" was in dispute. The Minisink settlers who came originally from New York were ignored by the New Jersey government, which claimed all land up to a point a little south of

Cochecton, and parceled the land among Jerseymen who came over the mountains, but the Dutchmen refused to give up their rights, hence friction. Numbers of the settlers were captured and lodged in Jersey prison houses; the men went armed at all times.

Between 1730 and 1740 several attempts were made to oust a Major Swartwout from his holdings. The Major was held in much local reverence as a model for all heroes, and spent a reasonable portion of his time telling of the awful things that would happen to the Jerseymen should they attempt to lay violent hands on him or his. But the enemy came in the night and the Major, in spite of all his bombast, was bundled out into the dew in a fashion that took all the brag out of him, while those of New Jersey made themselves at home in his mansion. However he was in command of the Orange County Militia, and gathering his cohorts around him he carried his one time castle by assault and the invaders were initiated into the walk known as Spanish then and there, the Major imparting sundry kicks in his efforts to give point to his advice as to where they should go and, as I understand it, it was not New Jersey that he recommended. After this a spy was regularly kept among the Jerseymen, and thus their invasive efforts were usually frustrated.

Then there was the Major's son-in-law, Harmanus Van Inwegen, who was also regarded as a prize by those of Jersey, and these peace disturbers next planned a raid for his capture, but word was brought by the spies and a call was sent to the clans to meet at the Van Inwegen house.

The call was answered by a goodly number and Major Swartwout assumed command as a matter of course. He arranged his forces in line of battle, placing the left wing in command of Van Inwegen, while to Jacob Cuddeback was given command of the right. The feather in the Major's cocked hat is said to have held itself, up to the point where the enemy appeared in sight, with a fierceness and ferocity that would have done credit to the helmet of Navarre. But as the invaders, led on by a Jersey constable, marched on the field, that feather seemed somehow to have lost much of its aggressive character; it is moreover intimated that the said constable was not quite so bumptious, nor was his attitude on horseback so strikingly aggressive as had been the case some minutes before. It must be confessed that to be the only mounted man in such an assembly and at such a moment would naturally make a modest person feel unduly conspicuous.

To tell the truth neither force seems to have expected to see such a formidable array on the other side, and as the distance gradually lessened and they came within gunshot of each other, the Jerseymen halted in uncertain array and a dread silence fell that, as the minutes passed, became extremely embarrassing. The fact is one was afraid and the other dasn't, and it only needed a very small event to turn the scale of battle either way. Fortunately for the home guard this was furnished by a son of the Major who, uncertain in the event of being ordered to shoot as to whether he should aim at the enemy or over its head, called to his father for instructions, whereupon the old gentleman, remembering the former raid on his home, roared back in a voice that shook the hills: "Kill them!"

This was too much for Jersey, whose sons had come over the mountain with no thought of being killed, and its ranks broke "like thin clouds before a Biscay gale", filled with consternation at the thought of such untimely end.

The Major's men, knowing the lay of the land, intercepted the retreating braves in a ravine about two miles back and turned the retreat into a rout. "The only life lost was that of the constable's horse, which fell at the first fire, giving its owner a lift in the world he had not calculated on, and landing him in a bunch of brambles."

New York returned home after running its legs off scaring Jersey, and that was the end of that.

It was not until 1753 that the next attempt was made. This time Jersey appeared before the house of Thomas DeKay and demanded his surrender. The householder, however, locked his front door and, going to an upper window, made snoots at the invaders who, not looking for such opposition, were nonplussed and retired in confusion, vowing they would get him next time.

The French and Indian War diverted both sides for some years and it was not until 1765 that the next and last raid took place. And this was indeed a bloody occasion, though no lives were lost. Now it was Major Johannes Westbrook who was selected as the victim and Sunday was the day of attack. All unsuspicious of the impending invasion, the community was attending divine worship in the Maghackemeck church, and when they sallied forth for the Sunday dinner they met a fight for which they had small stomach.

The church was surrounded and the enemy rushed down on the defenseless worshippers with a soul-piercing shout that made them think the Devil himself had come for them.

It being the Sabbath neither side would use weapons other than those furnished by the Lord, and coats and hats were soon off and there was as fine a shindy on as ever adorned an Irish holiday. Bloody noses and black eyes were the order of the day, for both sides were hard hitters. But this time those from the south were in such force that they overwhelmed their opponents and Major Westbrook was carried a prisoner over the mountain.

In 1767 commissions were appointed by the two colonies to run a boundary line, but owing to the bitterness of feeling they dared not attempt it, and it was some time later that the disputed territory was surveyed and about equally divided.

A log house in Port Clinton as it was when Hine passed through.

PORT JERVIS AND CARPENTER'S POINT.

In 1789 the present site of Port Jervis was known as Nahant and, while the town is modern—1826—having been made by the canal, it was included in the Minisink country and there is yet standing here the stone house of Martinus Decker, built possibly about 1759, when Martinus was married to Jenneke Westbrook, known as Johannes Decker's fort. This was burned out by the Indians on July 19, 1779, but the solid stone walls were not injured and in 1797 Johannes Decker repaired the place and it stands to-day, on Main Street, Germantown, as he left it. After burning this building the Indians separated, one party proceeding to Peter Coikendall's, where they stopped long enough to burn him out and then went on to Van Aukens, whose outbuildings were burned, but the house was not attempted, as Levi Paulding was in command here with troops.

Prof. John M. Dolph, who has made a close study of the subject, believes that the first attack by Brant and his Indians in their descent on this valley was on the Decker house, which they captured and burned. The Indians then divided, one party crossing the Neversink and raiding along its east bank while the other followed near the river, destroying farm buildings, the old church and the residences at what is now Tri States.

They then reunited at Fort Van Auken, which was attacked on the night of July 20, 1779, and it was on the following morning that old Jacobus Van Auken, looking out of an upper window to see if the besiegers had retired, was shot and killed by one of them.

When Count Pulaski was ordered from the Minisink country to South Carolina, this region was left practically defenseless and Joseph Brant, recognizing his opportunity, immediately planned an invasion of the Delaware River settlements. His force of Tories and Indians expected to surprise the sleeping inhabitants at night, but were delayed several hours and did not arrive until noon of July 20, 1779.

The palisaded house of Major Johannes Decker, on the east side of the Neversink, was burned. The women and children of the family (all those at home) were compelled to stand by and see the destruction, though none were harmed. Brant even went so far as to allow Mrs. Decker to save what she could from the blazing building and directed his Indians to carry what she brought out to a place of safety.

It is said that a reward had been offered by the British for the capture of the Major, and that one of the objects of Brant's raid was the earning of this reward. But fortunately the Major was away, attending a funeral at Fort Van Auken, and it was while returning from this that he came upon a party of Indians in a bend of the road and dashed through the surprised savages so quickly that they failed to even fire at him. Fearing to meet a larger party beyond, he wheeled and rode back through the same group and was wounded twice before clearing them.

Then the frightened horse plunged into a fallen tree and had to be deserted. The Major hid in a cave and crossed the mountain next morning to Finchville, where he found his son, one of the scholars who escaped when the teacher, Jeremiah Van Auken, was murdered.

The invaders next destroyed several houses, a mill and the schoolhouse, where they killed and scalped Jeremiah Van Auken, the teacher. There is an interesting story in connection with this that seems to be well corroborated. The school boys fled to the woods, but the girls stood in a helpless huddle about the body of their teacher, expecting every moment to be scalped, or at least carried off, when Brant himself came upon the group and placed a black mark upon the apron of each, telling the girls that if an Indian approached to hold it up and they would be safe. The girls appear to have kept their wits well, for they are said to have hunted up their brothers and placed them under their garments, and thus all were protected by the marked aprons. Brant had said that he did not make war on women and children.

It was after this that the attack was made on the Daniel Van Auken fort, on the present Laux farm, on the east side of the Neversink. This failed, two Indians being killed in the attempt, though, as previously stated, they managed to pot-shot old Jacobus at an upper window.

Brant's report of the raid made to Colonel Bolton is interesting. It was dated at Oquwage (Deposit), 29th July, 1779, and so far as relates to the destruction of the settlement is as follows:—

"I beg leave to acquaint you that I arrived here last night from Minisink and was a good deal disappointed that I could not get into that place at the time I wished to do—a little before daylight—instead of which I did not arrive until noon, when all the cattle was in the woods, so that we could get but a few of them. We have burned all the settlement called

Minisink, one excepted, round which we lay before about an hour and had one man killed and two wounded; we destroyed several small stockaded forts and took four scalps and three prisoners, but did not in the least injure women and children. The reason that we could not take more of them was owing to the many forts about the place, into which they were always ready to run like ground-hogs."

The Battle of the Minisink followed sharp on the heels of this raid. As soon as the news was carried to Goshen, such men as could hastily formed a company and marched over into the Minisink country to afford relief. But on the high bank of the Delaware, above Port Jervis, they were outmanœuvred by the Indians with disastrous results.

Lawyer Harrison W. Nanny has been at the history of this battle until he has knocked the legs off pretty much all the interesting little stories connected therewith, and about all one can say now without fear of contradiction, is that the whites were badly defeated and many were killed. It was some years ago that Mr. Nanny sprung this sad surprise, and we hope that his legal business has since become so extensive and exacting that he has had no more time to destroy our stories and legends.

As usual the settlers at first held such religious services as they could in private houses, but by 1736 the means were collected for the construction of four churches. The first, called the Mackhackemeck Church, was located about one-half mile south of where Port Jervis now stands and about one-half mile from the junction of the Delaware and Neversink Rivers, by the old burying ground. The second was about eight miles southwest from above, just around the bend in the road beyond Brick House, and was called the Minisink Church. The third was sixteen miles further on, in New Jersey, and was called the Walpack Church. The fourth was eight or ten miles distant from the Walpack and called the Smithfield Church— this on the Pennsylvania side of the river, near the Depue place. John Casparus Fryenmuth, Dutch Reformed, was the first pastor, and he covered the entire stretch. Preachers were scarce in those days and it seems that the settlement at Rochester made overtures to the Rev. Fryenmuth, which were resented by the Minisink flocks, and this is the way they voiced their sentiments:—

"Minisink, Dec. 6th, 1741.

"To the Rev. Consistory of Rochester, greeting:—

"We, your servants, having learned that you have had correspondence with our pastor, and have seduced him, so far as to send him a call, thinking that the large amount of salary promised him will induce him to leave us—the Lord who has thus far caused your acts of supplanting to fail will further direct them to a good end. We find ourselves bound to obey the command of the Saviour, 'Do good to them that hate you'; we therefore will deal with you hereafter, as we have before, 'doing you good'. It is true that you give us no thanks for his services among you. You are bold enough to say that he has eight free Sundays during the year, which is as true as the assertion of the Devil to Eve, 'You will not surely die'.

"If you desire, then, to have our minister four or six times during the year, we will grant your wish cheerfully, and leave it with our pastor to settle with you as to the amount of his compensation. If this cannot prevent the execution of your unjust intention, and the Lord wishes to use you as a rod to chasten us, we shall console ourselves with his gracious words, Heb. 12, 'Whom the Lord loveth he chasteneth, and he rebukes every son whom he adopts'. If it please the Lord to permit you to deprive us of our pastor, then we hope that your consciences will not be seared so much as to take away our livelihood, amounting to £125 12s 6d (overpaid salary).

"Should this, however, be the case, then we will not hesitate to give the matter into the hands of a worldly judge. We expect your answer, and conclude our discourse with the wish that the grace of our Lord and the love of God the Father, and the communion of the Holy Ghost, may remain with you until a blessed eternity. Amen. We remain your servants,

"John Cortright,
"John Van Vliet,
"Abm. Van Campen,
"William Cole."

It is about time to proceed with our tramp, but before we get too far away there is a little matter of a witch which should have our attention.

This was an ancient dame named Mollie Oldfield, who lived a solitary life (about one-half mile southwest of Millsburg, in the town of Minisink—in the matters of history it is well to be as accurate as possible), who came in time to be regarded as one "holding communion with the damned", and was dreaded and feared by the entire neighborhood; she pinched the children in their sleep and furnished every ill the countryside was heir to.

One day Captain Brown, having some business with the old lady, did not transact it to her liking, whereupon she pronounced his doom with, "Never mind, Captain Brown, you will be sorry for this some day", and the Captain was immediately sorry, for a great dread straightway filled all the vacant places in his top story. Soon his cows gave bloody milk, the Old Boy got into the churn and the butter refused to come; but the Captain knew a trick or two himself and, gathering all the horse shoes he could find—this was a desperate case, and one would hardly cover the job—he heated them red hot and plunged them in the cream, whereupon arose a great steam, against which no witch can stand (a too strong suggestion of the next sphere of action, possibly), and as the witch vanished the butter came.

Then there was the case of another neighbor, one James Neily, who crossed the path of the old lady at a wrong angle; the trouble here was also with his cattle, to whom the witch furnished wings that they might fly the coop, so to speak. And always did he find them in his fields of growing grain and no fences broken down, or any evidence of forcible entry. It did no good to watch; so long as a watch was kept nothing happened, but no sooner did James turn his back than over the fence his cattle flew again. But Neily, being possessed of a hard head and plenty of common sense, made friends with the mammon of unrighteousness in the person of Mrs. O., and his cattle thereafter remained within bounds.

The old woman's death was a tragic one, but one which she appears to have brought on herself. It seems that one day an inoffensive neighbor attempted to ride past her hovel on the old family mare, when the animal refused to pass the door in spite of all blows and known forms of speech, whereupon the rider, in the heat of argument, struck the horse on the head with a stone, killing her instantly. The next day a person entering this abode of darkness found the woman dead and blood issuing from her mouth and nose, and it was evident to all that she had for some reason taken possession of the mare and the blow that killed one killed both. So recently as

1887 one of the jury of inquest, then a very old man, was still living, and I understand these facts came first hand from him and are absolutely correct.

The trolley disposes of a mile or so to the outskirts of Port Jervis, setting us down at the entrance of the Carpenter's Point burial ground, and we walk down to the Tri-States' monument at the point for the sake of the view, so typical is it of the "Hudson River School" of a generation ago: a beautiful foreground of river with distant forest and more distant mountains fading off into the blue, and all framed with the branches of nearby trees, a spot to conjure dreams. The Indian name of the river was Keht-hanne, "the greatest stream"; also Lenapewihittuck, "the river of the Lenape". It was also known as the Minisink's River, which word means "Indians of the highlands", or "of the rocks".

On the outermost rock of all stands a low marker indicating the corner where New York, New Jersey and Pennsylvania come in touch with each other. While above it, on the bank, stands a stone which tells the traveler that this is the "Witness Monument, 1882. South 64 degrees, W. 72½ feet from this is the Tri State Rock, which is the Northwest end of the New York and New Jersey Boundary and the North end of the New Jersey and Pennsylvania Boundary", and again, "The corner between New York and Pennsylvania is in the center of the Delaware River, 475 feet due west of the Tri State Rock".

MONTAGUE.

"Minisink was that expanse of land lying west of the Shawangunk Mountains, about forty miles long by the same distance in width, including portions of Orange and Sullivan Counties, and of northern New Jersey", and we will now work our way back to the highway and proceed toward the discovery of its southernmost bound at Walpack Bend, or Flatbrookville.

After crossing the Neversink our way keeps well out of sight of the Delaware through the rich flat lands that in times past have been brought down from above and deposited here that those who live by the sweat of their brow might sweat to good purpose.

The highway is as dusty as a miller and not always the pleasantest place in the world for a tramp, but one is pretty sure to find a farmer going his way and to catch a ride if he wants it. Some two or three miles along and on the river side of the road stands the Van Auken house, which the present occupant, Mrs. F. E. Westfall, states was built by her great-great-great-grandfather, a Van Auken. The lady herself is of age to have grown children, so that counting twenty-five years to a generation, the building may be 175 years of age, which would carry it back to the days of border warfare between the inhabitants of the two provinces, and yet I cannot find that it is the nucleus of any tale or legend that can claim an age half so great.

The Tri-State Rock, so named because it actually is in three states—New York, New Jersey, and Pennsylvania.

Headstones of the old Minisink Burying Grounds have been all but obscured in myrtle for many years. If men were at work in the Pahaquarry Mines in 1650-1659, it is likely that the dead were taken to Shawnee, Pa., for burial. This Minisink cemetery (*above*) was bought and dedicated to the public in 1731. Below, the Van Auken house, from Hine's collection.

Next on the list come Shippekonk rocks, a smooth rock slide from the top of the ridge to the valley's floor. The name is Indian, and is also applied to an island in the river, but its meaning is hidden.

Some four or five miles below Carpenter's Point one comes on a small family graveyard in the corner of a field, and close on the right. Here lies Christopher Decker and his wife, grandparents of Mr. Demmon Reynolds, of Napanoch, whose "mother had relations enough killed by the Indians to make a nice little chunk of burying ground".

The Decker home, which stood nearby, was a refuge often sought by Tom Quick, the noted Indian slayer, and Mr. Reynolds's mother who, as a girl, was many times carried across the Delaware at Punkey's Rift in the arms of this hero of the countryside, has filled him o'er and o'er with stories which she heard recounted by the great man himself. Some of the legends current in these days Mr. R. knows are not so, because his mother never heard them from Tom—such as, for instance, the split log trap wherein Tom caught several Indians by their fingers. But many others are well authenticated, because this mighty hunter of the redskins told them on himself, and who should know better. The following story explains the reason for Tom's bitter hatred of the Indians and tells why and how he disposed of one of them.

The father of Tom Quick, a Hollander who immigrated to this country about 1733, was old and gouty, but he liked to see how the farm was coming on, and occasionally his two sons would help him out around the place. On one such occasion, when a considerable distance from the house, a party of Indians broke from the woods after them. The Quicks were unarmed, and could but run for it, so the boys took the old man, one on each side, and started for the house. Tom's brother was hit by a bullet, but not seriously hurt; but the father was heavy and helpless, and begged his boys to drop him and save themselves, else all would be slaughtered.

It was a hard sort of a proposition, but the arguments of the elder were perfectly sound, and the boys finally left him to his fate.

The Indians killed and scalped the old man, cut off his head and kicked it over the ground. Among the things taken from his body was a pair of silver knee buckles.

Long after, when peace had been declared, Tom Quick and some of his boon companions were drinking and playing cards in a tavern near where the village of Milford now stands, when an Indian, exhausted with cold and hunger, came in and begged for a drink. It was against the law to give an Indian liquor, but because of his condition they gave him a dram to take the chill off, and it was probably a hearty one, for the visitor soon showed signs of overindulgence and began to brag of his past deeds of prowess, displaying the buckles which Tom recognized as those taken from his father and saying over and over in a bragging tone, "Me Tom Quick, now; me Tom Quick, now".

The brutal way in which his father had been killed and the body treated had led Tom to swear never to let an Indian get away from him alive if he could help it, and Tom paid brutality with brutality, though aside from his treatment of the Indians and a fondness for drink he was well regarded by his neighbors.

When Tom saw those buckles and heard the insulting brag it aroused all his old-time hatred and he arose quietly from the table and walked toward the fireplace, over which hung a gun, but the landlord, divining his purpose, stopped Tom and reminded him that it was the closed season for Indians then and to kill the fellow in the house would cause serious trouble for all present.

The Indian had talked of how he was a mighty hunter and had given a promiscuous invitation to the company to go hunting with him, and now Tom accepted his offer. Of course, all knew what that meant—all but the Indian—and the two went off together. The snow was deep and Tom went on ahead to break a path, and while doing so heard the unsuccessful snap of the Indian's gun and, turning, asked what he had tried to shoot, to which the Indian responded "an eagle", and they went on.

Soon Tom claimed to be tired, and told the Indian to take his turn at breaking the path and, good, innocent soul that he was, the gentle savage did as requested, and it was not long before those at the tavern heard Tom's gun, and shortly thereafter saw him returning with the silver buckles.

Tom lived in a cabin in the woods in which he was one day trapped by the Indians, who for once had him off his guard. He was a captive beyond price, and they immediately concluded to take him to the headwaters of the Susquehanna and there build a great fire in honor of the event.

The snow was deep and the Indians had tramped long that day, and they concluded to remain in the cabin over night, so Tom's hands were tied and his moccasins taken from him, in the belief that he would not venture barefoot into the heavy drifts outside, and his captors lay down to sleep. Tom paced the floor like a caged lion, but every time he passed the door his elbow pushed up the wooden latch a bit until, as the Indians were about dropping off to sleep he had the door where one slight push would swing it open.

When the time seemed propitious Tom opened the door and started with a bound down hill. Some noise he made awakened the Indians, and they were after him almost instantly, and it was only a lucky accident that saved him. The day had been mild enough to cause some melting of the snow and this in turn had created a dense fog. Tom, being unable to see much of anything, tripped before he had gone far and fell, sinking deep into a drift. The pursuers were hot on his track, but overshot the mark, and as Tom lay still they finally gave up the search and he managed to wriggle out of his cool nest and eventually found his way to the Decker house, where it took three weeks to bring his frozen feet back to usefulness.

These stories do not agree very well with those published in the "Original Life and Adventures of Tom Quick"; in fact one of them is not to be found therein at all and the other combines incidents distributed between two separate tales in the book, but in view of the direct way in which they have been handed down from Tom himself and the intimate relations existing between the hero and the ancestors of Mr. Reynolds, it is reasonable to suppose that they are quite as likely to be correct as are the accounts hitherto published.

We are passing through the township of Montague, which is said to contain the most valuable land in the Minisink patent, and shortly come on Millville, where Chambers Brook performs after the manner of brooks that have been dammed from their youth up. There was not much room for a mill pond here, and as time went on the little pond evidently filled up, when the miller, instead of cleaning it out, built another dam higher up in the gap; at least that is the way it looks from the road to a stranger who finds no one handy by of whom to ask questions.

Millville is the site of a revolutionary blockhouse, and the knoll here is known as Block House Hill. Mr. Thomas J. Bonnell, of Port Jervis, tells me this was the headquarters of Capt. James Bonnell, who commanded at the Minisink during the Revolution. Mr. T. J. B. has an interesting manuscript book in which his ancestor, first a Justice of the Peace and later a Captain, kept his record of trials, copies of important letters, orders to the troops under him, petitions, etc.

Copies of a few of the more interesting of these are given below:—

Minisink 4th Apl. 1782.

Sir—Inclosed is a Return of Amunition wanting for my Company, I wish it may be forwarded with all Posib. dispatch, as it is a matter of the greatest Magnitude Occationed by the Enemies being Hourly expected to dis(?) our Frontiers, and my Amunition being nearly Exhausted—if you have any loose Powder I wish you'd send a few Pounds in Room of Cartridges for the Riflemen who scout the woods. I am Sir

Your very Humble Servt.
Ja. Bonnell, Capt.
Comd.g at Minisink.

Lt. Hamilton.

Minisink, 15th May 1782.

Sir

On monday the 4th Instant I summond you to Apeare before me at the House of Capt. Shimer the ss to answer the Complaint of Abraham Cuddeback, you neither appeared nor assignd any reason for your Nonattendence; I hereby Notify you that next Monday at twelve OClock at the House of Capt. Westbrook in Sandiston is the time and place Appointed for settling your dispute, and unless you attend you must Abide the Consequences of your neglect.

Sir your hum'l Servent

Ja: Bonnell.

Mr. Cox.

Minisink 15th May 1782.

Dear Sir

Yesterday three Indians was discovered on the Pennsylvania shore opposite to Walpack Capt. Hover imediately Persued them with a number of good Fellows. What sucksess I have not yet learnt; Pray let me know if you have made any discoveries of the Savages.

I am Sir

Your humble Servent

Ja: Bonnell.

Capt. Westfall
Comd.g at Peanpack.

Thursday Morning 4th July 1782.

This being the glorious Anniversary of American Independence The men of Capt. Bonnell's Compy will Parade this Afternoon Percisely at 4 O Clock, to Fire a Fudejoy on so Auspicious an Occasion.

The men will appear on Parade in the neatest manner Posible. Each man with his beard Clean shaved, hair neatly cut, clothes put on in the best order Possible, guns Perfectly Clean & a large green Bough in each Hatt—the least disobedience of this Order will meet with the most Serverest Punishment.

Ja: Bonnell Capt.
Comd.g at Minisink.

Minisink 10th December 1782.

His Excellency Governor Livingston and the Honourable Legislative Council, and General Assembly of New Jersey.

Gentlemen

We the Inhabitants of the Frontiers of the County of Sussex beg leave to Present our Petition to the Honourable Legislature of the State.

The Inhabitants who formerly lived on the Pennsylvania Side of the River Opposite to us have Principally left there Farms and Moved into Jersey and other places to Escape Savage Cruelty.

These Inhabitants was formerly a Considerable Guard to us, but now there is nothing to stop the Enemy but the River which is Fordable in a great Number of Places a Considerable part of the year, Particularly in Harvest and Other times when the Enemy Can do us the Greatest Dammage.

The Situation of this Country and the manner the savages Carry on the War like a Thief in the Night renders it Impracticable to depend on the Malitia for Security, for before they can be Collected the Mischief is done and the Enemy Secure in the Wilderness.

Numbers of us have Friends and near Relations who have ben Torn from there Families and Connections and are Groaning under Cruel Savage Captivity.

Others Labour under the Sad Remembrance of having experienced the Truly Shocking Spectacle of Seing there Dearest Connections Brutally Murderd and Scalped before there Eyes and we have grate reason to fear we shall share the Same Fate unless some mode be Addopted for our Security.

We therefore most earnestly pray that a Law may be passed by the Honourable Legislature before the Adjourn for raising a Company of about Eighty men Properly Officered and to be Stationed here for our Protection the ensuing Campaign.

signed by the inhabitants
& forwarded by Capt. Bonnell

It is but a brief step now to Montague and Brick House, which latter is the name generally used on guide boards. Brick House was built in 1776 by Roger Clark of bricks of an odd size that were manufactured within three-quarters of a mile of the spot, and from the beginning was a noted stopping place. For a long time the New York to Oswego stage made this one of its regular places of call.

Judge James Stoll tried for many years to get possession of the place, but he and Clark never agreed very well and the latter refused to sell. So the Judge persuaded a Philadelphia liquor dealer to buy the inn for him, and Clark readily fell into the trap. The Judge wished a patch of land alongside for a garden, and this the Philadelphian insisted on. Once the bargain was made, the Judge shortly came into possession, and though he never ran the place himself, he always made a bargain with his tenant-landlord that the latter buy all his liquor from the store run by Stoll across the road.

The road running straight away from the front of the Brick House is the old stage route to Deckertown and Jersey City.

In 1774 there stood on the site of the Brick House an old log cabin occupied by Daniel Decker and his vrouw Grietje. One June day as the latter stood in the meadow in front of her home, engaged in boiling soap, Daniel the Valiant came rushing by with a wild cry of "Indians! Indians!" and exhorting his good woman to escape as best she could, himself crawled into a hollow log through a knothole of which he could safely gaze on the coming trouble. But the woman was made of sterner stuff and calmly continued her soap boiling, when shortly two redskins appeared on the scene, and with nothing more dangerous in view than a woman they approached, scalping knife in hand, each anxious to secure the prize.

Grietje stood her ground apparently unaware of her impending doom, until the headmost foe was almost on her when, turning suddenly with a ladle of boiling soap, she dashed it squarely in his face and he put up a howl which gave the best of evidence that he felt hurt, and turned himself to the nearby brook for comfort—that same brook that to-day gurgles pleasantly past the end of the Brick House. His companion, not understanding such mode of warfare nor appreciating the force of the woman's argument, and only noting that a kind Providence had intervened in his behalf and that the scalp was his for the lifting, came promptly forward and received a like application that took all the starch out of him, and he in turn interviewed the brook.

If the savages did not enjoy it, neither did they quite understand this new method of treatment, but they had acquired a healthy respect for Grietje, and stood afar off while they wondered what had happened to them. For some time they debated the situation, but finally concluded that discretion was their best card, and after firing the cabin they disappeared in the woods.

When the danger was all over, the lord of creation crawled out of his hole, and approached his better half with a light remark to such effect as, "Didn't we fix 'em, though?" Now, the old lady was in no mood for trifling and, turning savagely on Daniel, she gave him a dipper filled to the brim with that boiling soap—at least she gave him the soap, keeping the dipper for further argument, if need be—and remarking at the same time: "There, you old fool; go and lay in your holler log till you get cooled off, you old coward, you. I'll teach you!" and Daniel he went, not for the hollow log, but for that blessed stream, which for the third time that day proved to be balm and healing.

A new cabin was soon built, but opposite to the old one, and "Uncle Dan'l" drew a picture of Grietje in the act of dousing the Indians, which for years graced its walls; but in 1793, the old couple being dead, the cabin was pulled down and the picture was lost.

As before mentioned, one of the series of early churches built in Minisink was located here, just around the bend of the road beyond the Brick House. It is told locally of the Rev. Elias Van Benschoten, called in 1785 to be pastor of the three Dutch churches of Machackemech, Minisink and Walpack, that when preaching his farewell sermon to this congregation the peroration concluded with, "Hogs I found you, hogs I leave you, and the Devil may receive you". It would appear as though the old gentleman was not in an altogether amiable frame of mind at the moment.

There is a story current concerning Major Nyce and Polly Hoornbeck, which, if I have it correctly, runs something like this: The Major, when a young man, counted Polly among his friends and was wont to call on her occasionally, but he never seems to have hit it up very swift and one night Polly, who was sitting on the opposite side of the fireplace from him, began to jerk herself and say, "Stop, now; leave me alone". The young man looked on in a maze for a few moments, but finally managed to blurt out: "Why, Polly, what's the matter with you? I ain't a techin' you." "Well", responds the girl, "you devilish fool; if you ain't a-going to you better go home". It is not recorded that the gentleman left immediately.

As our road continues south it is not quite so much of a traveled highway, though one can still kick up a good deal of dust as far as Dingman's Ferry under average conditions.

A mile or so south of Brick House, and in the field north of and adjoining the residence of the brothers Black, lies "Spook Hollow". It is now cultivated ground, but within memory was wooded and a place of mystery and fear to young and old. One graybeard tells how, in his youthful days, he pattered past as fast as a pair of short legs would take him, lest a witch might get him; but he never had any actual encounter, nor did any of his friends, so far as he knows.

This was undoubtedly one of those secret places in the woods where, once on a time, the devils met with the would-be witches at midnight, there together to feast and dance. Through the air at such times would come coursing panthers, wolves and lesser terrors, from over hills, mountains and valleys. Toads and serpents were on hand to be worshipped, and just before day broke, and after signing their souls over to the Evil One, the witches were endowed with power to rule and ruin their fellow men.

Small wonder that Spook Hollow was passed in haste by honest folk.

"Ye hag is astride
This night, for to ride,
The Devil and she together.
Through thick and through thin,
Now out and now in,
Though ne'er so foul be the weather.

"A thorn or a burr
She takes for a spur
With the lash of a bramble she rides now

Through brakes and through briars
O'er ditches and mires
She follows the spirit that guides now."

—Robert Herrick.

A sad case of undeluding is said to have happened to a true believer, whose wife went on a visit to Esopus many, many years ago.

From the very start her man had trouble with the cows; they insisted on kicking him and treating him in a most disrespectful manner, and when he tried to churn, the butter positively refused to come. So he called in his friend, the witch doctor, who builded an altar of stones in the barnyard and cast a spell over it. He then by incantations discovered that the absent wife was a witch, who had put a spell on cattle and churn when she left, and warned the husband not to allow the woman inside the house until she promised on the Bible not to have anything more to do with the Devil.

Now the wife returned in due course and when her husband explained the situation to her, she, after one look at the cattle, thus remarked: "You old fool, the cows have the kine-pox; the butter would not come because you put no hot water in it, and I would just like a tomahawk and scalping knife to go for that quack doctor. I am going into my house in spite of your witch spell and the Devil"—and in she went, and first thing she did was to cure her husband, and while the process is said to have been painful to a degree, it is understood to have been thoroughly effective; after which she took the cows in hand.

The Brick House Hotel as Hine saw it (*above*) and as it appeared in more recent years (*below*). Removed several years ago for a traffic circle and another crossing of the Delaware River, this old inn, erected in 1776 in Montague Township, opposite Milford, Pa., continued operation until the mid-1950's. Demolitionists found flintlock muskets in a secret cupboard.

The Isaac Van Campen house, Schapanach, in Hine's day (*above*) and at a later time (*below*). Built about 1750, it served as an inn for celebrated guests such as John Adams, journeying from Massachusetts to sessions of the Congress in Philadelphia. More than 150 men, women, and children found refuge here in 1763 when under Indian siege. Count Pulaski camped here in what is now Wallpack Township, Sussex County, as did General Gates with seven regiments.

SANDYSTON AND WALPACK.

Some quarter of a mile below Spook Hollow stands a building known as the "Fort", a simple one-story-and-attic dwelling whose loopholes for muskets still gape on those outside its walls.

Here in the early days settled Johannis Westbrook on one side of the little stream which divided the towns of Montague and Sandyston, while on the other side was reared the home of Daniel Westfall. The one still standing is the house of Captain Westbrook, in Sandyston, mentioned in the second letter of "Ja: Bonnell", quoted above.

This, I presume, is the stone fort known as Nomanoc, and was undoubtedly the rallying point for some little distance up and down the river. It was from here that Capt. Peter Westbrook sallied forth with his men to the battle of the Raymondskill, or Conashaugh, April 21, 1780, which was fought just over the river in Pennsylvania where the Captain, Lieutenant Ennis and twelve others were killed. Those remaining retreated below Cave Bank, and the place is called Death Eddy to this day. Another account places the battle in 1778, says that Captain Westbrook escaped badly wounded to a canoe, and that two or three men of the expedition were lost.

It was also from this fort that seven men went out to death while in the performance of duty. Word had been brought in that Indians were in the neighborhood and a party of scouts was sent out. These found in the light snow moccasined footprints near the river bank at Death Eddy, and while they were bunched and in the act of examining them the Indians, who were ambushed behind the bank, shot and killed the entire party. This was about a half mile below the fort.

About 1739 the most important settlement in the valley was located here, opposite Minisink and Nomanoc Islands. A public school was established in 1731.

The roadmakers have a way of running highways in as straight a line as the nature of the ground will permit, and as the flat lands on this east side of the Delaware are quite extensive above Dingman's, the road gives the impression of deliberately avoiding the river as much as possible, even running over the toes of the hills to do so, and all the traveler knows about the river here is what the map says.

Several stone houses are passed that suggest a possibility of stories and things, but if there are such they are a sealed book, and we will keep on down the highway. Dingman's Ferry is now a modern iron bridge that is merely useful, and we pass on without even a look and begin the climb over the ridge that in days long gone took quite a fall out of the river. It must have been a good deal like rolling out of one of those old-fashioned, four-post bedsteads that required a stepladder introduction. But the ridge has been worn through until now it hardly causes a ripple of excitement.

But the wayfarer still has a long hill to pull over, known here as Pompey Ridge—below as Walpack Hill. On one occasion this traveler found himself near the top of the hill as night was coming on, and kept on over into Peters Valley, adjoining, where was bed and board at Bevens P. O.

Those who cater to the needs and comfort of the public here are not early risers. My landlady announced that the morning meal might happen any time between 6 and 7 o'clock. As a matter of fact it did not happen until nearly 8; there was plenty of it, though, and reasonably good for the price, one dollar for supper, bed and breakfast. When the meal was ready the good woman went into the bar and thumped on the ceiling with the broom, and in due course her men came trooping down stairs. Dressing consisted of getting into trousers, shirt and shoes, and did not take long.

Once back to the hilltop from the place of my night's lodging, I found the down grade of the river road quite as long as the upward climb of last evening, but it's down. The views from both slopes include mountain and river and are always beautiful. Sometimes one strikes the eye more forcibly, sometimes the other; it depends largely on atmospheric conditions and how the shadows lie, but the southern slope, it seems to me, furnishes a more varied assortment of foregrounds—at least such is the impression that remains.

And then this down grade carries one to the very edge of the river, even if it is only for a moment, and right here is a spot where I came on a clump of wild flowers or escapes that were altogether different from old acquaintances in the line, one to two feet high and perched on the end of the stem; the petals started in green and continued to the end in the most brilliant scarlet, lighting up the meadow in quite as brilliant fashion as does England's poppy.

We are on the outposts of Schapanach. October 15, 1735, Adam Dingman purchased land here. And here lay the farm of John Cleves Symmes, who about 1760 removed from Long Island to these western wilds. His wife, Anna, mother-in-law of President Harrison, lies in the old burial ground on the hill at the left as we go. It was John Cleves, Jr., who was the author of the theory that the north pole was a hole in the ground.

The log church, Dutch, erected previous to the Revolution at this point, was in use as late as 1826. Just below this burial ground formerly stood, on the lower end of the knoll which commands an extended view up and down the river, the old fort erected during the French and Indian War and which, during the Revolution, was part of the dwelling of Col. John Rosenkrans.

The old stone house still standing just under and south of this knoll was probably built by Isaac Van Campen, member of the Legislature from 1782 to 1785. An iron fireback made for the house at the Oxford Furnace bears date 1742. About 1811 this property was purchased from Abraham Van Campen by Henry De Witt, of Rochester, for his son John H. DeWitt, who built the peculiar long-roofed barn still standing. When in 1829 slavery was abolished in New Jersey, the only slave in Sussex County was Cæsar, belonging to the De Witts here; he refused his freedom.

In 1776 a band of prowling Indians captured three Walpack settlers, McGinnis, Teal and Courtright, in broad day and escaped across the river into the wilds of Pennsylvania before the alarm was given.

Capt. Emmanuel Hoover immediately gathered a party of men and started in pursuit. The Captain was an eminently efficient leader and all were thorough woodsmen; as the savages were trailed scouts were thrown ahead to prevent a surprise. It was not long before McGinnis was found murdered and scalped, and this spurred on the pursuers who, by care and expedition, came on the unsuspicious savages preparing their camp for the night.

In the midst of the camp the other prisoners could be seen tied hand and foot, and Hoover gave his men directions to surround the camp, and after all were asleep to close in on a given signal, but under no circumstances to fire a gun until the signal was given. As the hours crept on the net was drawn closer and closer and the time had almost arrived for the attack when an Indian arose to replenish the fast dying fire. The sight so aroused the fury of a friend of the murdered McGinnis that he forgot everything in his desire for revenge and shot the Indian dead. The camp was of course in instant commotion, the warriors merely staying long enough to attempt the killing of their prisoners, and then plunged into the outer darkness where further pursuit was out of the question.

The bonds were cut and the released men hurried away from the dangerous firelight before inquiry was made as to their condition, when it was found that Teal had escaped unhurt, while Courtright was severely wounded.

There was now nothing to do but return home with the one red scalp when they should have had those of all the party, and shouldering their wounded neighbor the return journey was made as quickly as possible. (Above is condensed from an account written in 1879 by W. H. Layton, who stated that he had the facts from a sketch written by a grandson of Andrew Dingman.)

From now on to Flatbrookville a succession of woodland and river views follow each other in beautiful profusion. The scent of the wild strawberry burdens the air, if it be mid June, while great masses of laurel bloom, or the more scattered clusters of rhododendron border the way.

We pass a rustic watering trough, and next a ruined log house, and just as the road is about to swing onto the river's edge and at the foot of an enormous double tree on the west, wells a spring of pure cold water that is a great find for the thirsty traveler—a plank step through the fence shows the way.

Here is the most beautiful river view of the entire trip. The bank, which the road follows closely at this point, is bordered by great trees whose branches frame the loveliest of pictures of mountain and stream, rocks and sandy points, with possibly a lone fisherman enjoying his vacation idle.

This part of the road is but little used, at one spot so overgrown is it with weeds that it is undecipherable, but a few feet in advance, and so dense is the thicket on the riverside that the water is hardly to be seen. An emerald tunnel through primeval woods where the scarlet tanager flits, and walled in places with the rhododendron.

"Glooms of the live-oaks, beautiful-braided and woven
With intricate shades of the vines that myriad-cloven
Clamber the forks of the multiform boughs,—
Emerald twilights,—
Virginal shy lights,
Wrought of the leaves to allure to the whisper of vows,
When lovers pace timidly down through the green colonnades
Of the dim sweet woods, of the dear dark woods,
Of the heavenly woods and glades
That run to the radiant marginal sand-beach within
The wide sea-marshes of Glynn;—

"Beautiful glooms, soft dusks in the noon-day fire,—
Wildwood privacies, closets of lone desire,
Chamber from chamber parted with wavering arras of leaves,—
Cells for the passionate pleasure of prayer to the soul that grieves,

Pure with a sense of the passing of saints through the wood,
Cool for the dutiful weighing of ill with good;—"

—Sidney Lanier.

Finally there comes a point where one must cross the Walpack Hill or take the long way around to Flatbrookville, and if it is the far end of the day, when every half mile counts, it's likely you would go over the hill as I did. At first our uplift is an interesting woods road where the shade is very grateful on a warm day and where all manner of wild flowers abound. A stiff climb for a half mile or so.

Then comes a crossroad with a farmhouse and a suggestion of cultivation, then some up-and-downness, and finally the decline to Flat Brook, a trout stream of no mean reputation.

Flatbrookville has a back-woods flavor that immediately appeals to one. The stream is harnessed to a little saw and grist mill, there is here a hotel and a store, and a few houses that straggle down the road in a casually careless sort of fashion. The talk is of fish and fishing and the farmers complain that the deer eat up their garden truck.

From an address delivered by Mr. B. B. Edsall, at the Sussex County Centenary, we learn that the first settlement in the county was that along our Old Mine Road. That in 1738 the only grist mill in the county was on Flat Brook near the Delaware River, and that one of the first three saw mills in the county was on Flat Brook. That in 1738 the county contained not more than 5-600 inhabitants, and that wagons were then unknown in Sussex save in the Minisink region.

At the mouth of the brook in the Delaware is the remarkable whirlpool, the Indian name of which, Wahlpeck, meaning whirlpool, gives name to the township according to Heckewelder. Mr. Ruttenber says that it is probably a corruption of Walpeek, meaning "deep water", and was formerly the name of a lake.

The hotel boasts an indolent old cat that can furnish a ten-minute entertainment to guests whenever she wishes. It appears that tabby is very fond of lying in the dust of the road, but no sooner does she settle down than the barn swallows proceed to have fun with her ladyship—it can be nothing else. The birds swoop down within an inch or less of pussy's whiskers, causing her at times to jump back from the too close contact. Occasionally she makes a quick move with intent to intercept their flight, but by the time her paw is out the bird is fifty feet hence, and finally Mistress Pussy, unable to stand it longer, retires to cover. I saw the operation twice repeated and was told that it was of frequent occurrence and that never yet, so far as known, had one of the birds been caught.

The first mail route, 1852, was established from Flatbrookville to Newton my way of Millbrook, Hardwick and Stillwater.

Two views of the Old Mine Road—as the author saw it (*above*) and more recently (*below*). Unless the traveler was careful, even in the days of the road's improvement, he would travel in a circle for hours if he did not make the right turn at Flatbrookville. In a tiny graveyard near this quiet stretch (*below*) is the headstone of Anna Symmes, mother-in-law of President William Henry Harrison.

Down from Flatbrookville and just across the Warren County line, Millbrook (*above*) was a thriving village seventy years ago with a church, mills, blacksmith shop, and stores—and, of course, a hotel. Comparatively few residents remain to enjoy its charm, viewed here from near the Appalachian Trail. This house (*below*) near Millbrook was once the home of Major Moses Van Campen. From Hine's collection.

PAHAQUARRY.

Our road, after crossing Flat Brook, immediately begins the ascent of the Kittatinny Mountain, which is the New Jersey continuation of old Shawangunk, and soon one is in a position to look down on Walpack Bend, or down stream as far as the atmosphere will allow.

The first crossroad carries the traveler along the side of the hill and may be the original mine road, but the interest lies in the village of Millbrook and along the banks of Vancampens Brook, as the map calls it, and it is thus we will go.

There are only two villages in the entire township of Pahaquarry, which is nothing but a side hill anyway, and Millbrook is one of them. Here in 1839 came Coonrad Welter, known to his neighbors as "Coon". His house soon became a home for all the circuit riders and preachers who visited the place, and was known as the "Methodist Tavern". Some of the circuits covered a five hundred mile trail, and the preachers commonly carried a tin horn with mighty blasts from which they announced their arrival.

There was no church building here until 1860.

The brook is a very pleasant companion as it ambles along down its little valley, until it takes to jumping the rocks, when it sounds from the road as though it was going all to smash; however, we catch it a little later dodging under the highway in such manner as would indicate that it can be entirely cheerful under the most adverse conditions.

Shortly after leaving Mill Brook to waste its substance on the Delaware we come on an old Van Campen house, built something less than two hundred years ago; its exact age is lost in the mist, but it was erected by a Van Campen, and Abraham Van C., the first, came to the Pahaquarry flats about 1720.

It is related that in the Spring of 1780 Major Moses Van Campen, who was born in this house, was captured by Indians with intent to take him to the headwaters of the Susquehanna, or some other inaccessible region, and there make a holiday of him, but apparently the captors did not figure on the Major's disinclination to be roasted and scalped.

The story, as abbreviated from the "Life of Van Campen", is as follows: After the Wyoming massacre such inhabitants as escaped spent their spare time in those forts which were nearest to their farms, but the temptation to return and cultivate the farms was strong within them. Thus the Major, with his father and younger brother, an uncle and cousin, and one Peter Pence, left Fort Wheeler, near Wyoming, for their clearings four miles distant. They were surprised, the father and brother murdered and scalped before his eyes and the Major himself taken prisoner; on the adjoining farm his uncle was killed and the boy and Peter Pence taken prisoners.

Then came the march toward Niagara, but before going far the family of one Pike was captured. The wife and child were allowed to go after being deprived of most of their clothing, but Pike was taken along with the others.

Van Campen had mixed with Indians all his life and knew them well, he was the bravest of the brave, had been with Sullivan when the Iroquois country was raided, and because of his character and ability was usually selected for the post of danger. He had at one time invaded a camp of sleeping Indians, counted those around one camp fire, counted the number of camp fires and escaped without detection, though the redskins numbered some seven hundred.

In his present position his thoughts naturally turned toward escape, and he began counselling his fellow prisoners with that end in view, but they could only see that they were three unarmed men against ten armed foes, and in order to arouse them to the situation Van Campen reminded his friends that they, being the first prisoners taken after the Sullivan raid, would undoubtedly be subjected to torture, and that they might better give up their lives in an attempt to escape, rather than supinely wait for such a terrible end, but even then it devolved on him to make all the plans.

His idea was to take the first opportunity that offered while their captors slept and take them at a disadvantage, and planned to have Pence station himself by the guns, which were always stacked about a tree, while he and Pike, with hatchets, should dispatch as many as possible before the enemy could assume the offensive.

The captives were tied every night, but while they were lying about the fire one evening, an Indian dropped a knife which the Major covered with his foot, and when all were asleep he worked his way out carefully and with the knife cut the bonds of his companions who, in turn, cut his. Pence immediately placed himself by the stacked guns, Pike with a hatchet was placed where he could quickly brain two of the savages, and Van Campen where he could kill three; but just at this critical moment the two assigned to Pike stirred and he, losing his nerve, lay down, but the Major recognized the situation as one calling for dispatch and quickly buried his hatchet in the heads of the two half-aroused men and then turned to the three originally set apart for him. As he struck down the last of these Pence opened fire with the guns and killed four.

Now there was but one left and he, not fully comprehending the situation, sprang for the guns and then, discovering his error, turned and fled for the cover of the woods with Van Campen close upon him. The latter raised his hatchet to strike, but missed the Indian's head and buried the blade in his shoulder. At the same instant both slipped and fell and grappled on the ground as they were; then came a struggle of giants. The blood from his foe's wound blinded the Major and put him at a disadvantage, but knowing that the Indian was feeling for his scalping knife and that quick action was required, he caught his toes in the belt of his adversary and with a mighty shove broke his hold and threw him several feet. The moment spent in searching for the hatchet gave the Indian an opportunity to reach the cover of the dark woods and the fight was over. Nine had been killed and one wounded man escaped.

Under such conditions the firelight was always dangerous and the three men gathered the booty as quickly as possible and retired to the cover of darkness to await the coming of day when they could with safety, take up their march for home. The booty consisted of twelve guns, one of which was Van Campen's own, blankets, coats, the nine Indian scalps and two white scalps which had been taken early in the raid.

In later years the Indian who escaped met Van Campen and identified himself by the scar in his back. Both were notable men among their kind, strong and courageous, and it is said they became good friends.

The Moravian Memorials quote Albert G. Broadhead as

authority for the statement that John Adams, while attending Congress in Philadelphia, as late as 1800, used the Old Mine Road as a link in the most eligible route from Boston to that city. "He was accustomed to lodge at Esquire Van Campen's in the Jersey Minisink". The general opinion seems to be that it was at this Van Campen house that Adams stopped, though if I understand it aright the Minisink only reached so far south as Walpack Bend, and if so it may have been at the Van Campen house in Shappanack.

There is yet another old stone house as I tramped, but it has been modernized to meet the needs of the Summer boarder and only its stout stone walls remain to suggest a tale. This was the home of Henry Shoemaker, a soldier of the Revolution. It seems that there was in this region an over enthusiastic, though it would appear a highly indiscreet, Tory, one Jim Barton by name.

Now Barton was unwise enough to hit a bigger man than himself with highly disastrous results. One night he waylaid and insulted Shoemaker, who climbed down from his horse and thrashed the Tory until he cried enough. But while the captor was willing to drop this line of argument he was not through, for he made Barton march down the road ahead of him to the house of George Michaels where the two fitted out their guest with a suit of tar and feathers and allowed him to depart in peace.

The objective of all these many pages is the Mine Holes of Pahaquarry, and we have come to them, but before proceeding with our own investigation, it may be well to introduce a few notes on the subject of mining in this region taken from a paper read before the Minisink Valley Historical Society, by Mr. J. H. Wood, on February 28, 1889.

Mr. Wood states that there existed a tradition handed down from the Indians that lead could be found on Tibb's Meadow tract, a half mile south of Culver's Gap in Sandyston. About thirty-five years ago some work was done here by Joseph Layton, but he was apparently unsuccessful, and abandoned the project.

Some seven miles south of this are signs of copper. Deeds of some one hundred acres here made in 1748 and 1759 mentioned a copper mine, the location of which is now unknown.

Two miles south of Walpack Center is an excavation under a large rock, showing traces of silver ore, and on an adjoining farm are veins of copper, which can be traced for some ten or eleven miles to the old copper mines of Pahaquarry.

One supposed to be posted has stated that one of the old mine holes of Pahaquarry was never made by a miner, as it was contrary to all rules and would entail a heavy expense to miss the vein a foot.

B. B. Edsall, deceased, "the best informed historian in the county of Sussex", said the pioneer settlement of Pahaquarry was made by Hollanders as early as 1664, and possibly prior to that date.

So much for what Mr. Wood dug out. The location of the copper mine holes is near Shoemaker's old "Union Hotel", about half way between Walpack Bend and the Water Gap, on Mine Brook, and it was here that our road terminated.

When I first came this way, in the Spring of 1907, there was a great noise of blasting. The price of copper was up and some gentleman of persuasive ways, believing that the mining of this ore would pay, started a company, sold stock and erected buildings containing much machinery, when, lo! the price of copper dropped and another dream was busted.

One of the old mine holes, excavated on a slant to minimize flooding.

A mine hole near the end of the Old Mine Road. From the author'
photograph.

Now all is as quiet as it was after the Dutchmen got through two hundred and fifty years ago. The two mine holes are a few hundred feet up the small brook that seems quite happy again now that the mercenaries are gone. The two holes are two holes from my point of view and that is about all there is to be said of them. No one knows who the original miners were, but the supposition is that they were some of the earliest Dutch explorers who disappeared long enough before the first actual settlers came to leave no memory or legend of themselves that is founded on anything more substantial than air. The surroundings are romantic and beautiful in the extreme, and it is a wonderful spot for a person with a well-trained imagination, provided he is careful not to sit down on a rattlesnake.

Just below is the scow ferry which takes the traveler across to Shanoe, where still stands the house of Nicholas Depue, who came this way about 1720, a man who is frequently mentioned in the old records.

When the rivers were frozen there was a good road from the mine holes to Esopus, over which (1730) wheat and cider were carried out and salt and necessaries brought back. Possibly our Old Mine Road at this time was little more than a bridle path.

When a navigable channel was opened through Foul Rift and it was possible to get out by boat, trade turned down stream and the road became less and less traveled.

The remaining miles to the Water Gap on the Jersey side keep in fairly close touch with the river; there is some cultivable land, all of which is taken advantage of for the purpose of keeping alive the Summer boarder. One Worthington owns a stretch about so wide and some two miles long which includes all the hilltop and has been turned into a deer park. This is all very nice and interesting for Mr. W., but a few Winters back when he found it difficult to feed his animals he calmly broke down his fences and turned the hungry and undiscriminating creatures loose on the farmers—at least, so the farmers say—and they do not appear to like it even to a small degree, for there is no open season in New Jersey for the killing of deer, and nothing pleases a deer better than a vegetable garden.

The highway for a mile along here is a quiet woodland road bordered with rhododendron and retaining the damp of the deep woods long after all else is dry and dusty; now and then some small brook does a fancy tumble or the waters drip from the moss-covered rocks.

As we come opposite the buildings which make the Gap settlement it has been found necessary to shave off the rocks in order to make way for the road. Still further down the water washed the base of a cliff so steep that even the Indian could not scale its face. This is still known as "Indian Ladder" because they here used a tree which leaned against the rock face by which to ascend. This was replaced later by the whites with a rope ladder, but the spot was always regarded as a dangerous one, until the engineer came with his drills and dynamite.

We have not only come to the end of our journey, but have run past it by some miles, for one must get home about a certain time in order to earn another vacation, and it's down here that the railroad is.

INDEX

This volume is a facsimile of Hine's Annual for 1908, entitled *History and Legend, Fact, Fancy and Romance of the Old Mine Road, Kingston, N. Y., to the Mine Holes of Pahaquarry.* In the original edition, photographs were mounted by hand, and they varied in number and subject from one copy to another. In this reissue, many of the original illustrations have been reproduced and others added, together with a new introduction by Henry Charlton Beck.

Milton Keynes UK
Ingram Content Group UK Ltd.
UKHW041004061024
2024UKWH00009B/12

9 780813 504278